OTHER BOOKS BY ELISABETH KÜBLER-ROSS
AND DAVID KESSLER

Life Lessons

OTHER BOOKS BY ELISABETH KÜBLER-ROSS

Why Are We Here (Germany)
Longing to Go Back Home (Germany)
Making the Most of the In-Between (Poland)
Unfolding the Wings of Love (Germany)
The Tunnel and the Light
On Life After Death
AIDS: The Ultimate Challenge
On Children and Death
Remember the Secret
Working It Through
Living with Death and Dying
To Live Until We Say Good-Bye
The Dougy Letter (Letters to a Dying Child)
Death: The Final Stage of Growth
Questions and Answers on Death and Dying
On Death and Dying
The Wheel of Life

OTHER BOOKS BY DAVID KESSLER

The Needs of the Dying

ON GRIEF
AND GRIEVING

Finding the Meaning of Grief
Through the Five Stages of Loss

Elisabeth Kübler-Ross
and David Kessler

SCRIBNER
New York   London   Toronto   Sydney

SCRIBNER
1230 Avenue of the Americas
New York, NY 10020

SCRIBNER and design are trademarks of Macmillan Library Reference USA, Inc.,
used under license by Simon & Schuster, the publisher of this work.

For information about special discounts for bulk purchases,
please contact Simon & Schuster Special Sales: 1-800-456-6798
or business@simonandschuster.com

DESIGNED BY ERICH HOBBING

Text set in Granjon

Manufactured in the United States of America

1   3   5   7   9   10   8   6   4   2

Library of Congress Cataloging-in-Publication Data

Kübler-Ross. Elisabeth.
On grief and grieving : finding the meaning of grief through the five stages of loss /
Elisabeth Kübler-Ross and David Kessler.
p. cm.
1. Grief. 2. Loss (Psychology). 3. Bereavement—Psychological aspects.
I. Kessler, David, 1959– II. Title.
BF575.G7K82 2005
155.9'37—dc22
2005042694

ISBN-13: 978-0-7432-6628-4
ISBN-10: 0-7432-6628-5

For my beloved granddaughters,
Emma Sadie and Sylvia Anna,
who kept me going when I kept going.
—Elisabeth

For two dear friends,
Berry Berenson Perkins and Wayne Hutchinson;
love never dies.
—David

Contents

CONTENTS

CONTENTS

Authors' Note

There is no correct way or time to grieve. We wrote this book hoping to familiarize the reader with the aspects of grief and grieving. No book should be used to replace professional help if that is needed. We hope this book will become a beacon by shedding light, hope, and comfort on the most difficult time we will all experience in our lives.

ELISABETH KÜBLER-ROSS
AND DAVID KESSLER
AUGUST 2004

Preface: "I Am Done"

On August 24, 2004, Elisabeth Kübler-Ross died. I looked up at the clock after her last breath and noted the time of death at 8:11 P.M. I have to say that if I hadn't seen it for myself, I might not have believed it. Apparently I wasn't the only one. Many people agreed that in some way they thought she was immortal. She always said that when she "transitioned and graduated," it would be cause for celebration since she would be "dancing in the galaxies among the stars."

For those of us who were very close to her, though, it was a loss. I will miss the feisty, funny, kind, and brilliant person I spent time with over the years. The loss of Elisabeth is a complex grief to me. She was a complex woman, so it was no surprise the grief I felt seeing her die day by day, piece by piece, was extremely challenging. At times during our writing, she would seem tired, but then she would suddenly perk up if something we wrote didn't quite flow.

She loved to teach. She always wanted to do more. She had a sharp mind when it came to her work. I am glad she enjoyed her work. Now that she is gone, I miss her terribly. And yet I know that in her death, she has found the freedom she could not find in life. She is no longer confined to a room, a bed, and a body that no longer works.

When I began this book with Elisabeth, she told me, "You

will have to go into grief yourself, if this book is to become all that it should be."

I obediently said, "Of course," suddenly flashing on old losses. I thought I was being directed to reexamine them. Then curiously I asked her, "Will you be going into your own grief also?"

"Naturally," she responded. "I have been in anticipatory grief for a long time now and I expect there is more to come." Thus was born the introduction to this book.

As we wrote the various sections, I did reflect on my own losses; how could I not? Thinking about grief naturally brought up my own, and as I sat with Elisabeth, she would grow emotional during parts of the writing as well. Her tears were a sign that she was visiting old wounds too. There is a saying that if your writing doesn't keep you up at night, it will never keep anyone else up at night either. In creating this book I often felt that if it didn't make us cry, if it didn't help us heal our own grief, it would never help anyone else.

I always left Elisabeth after a session of writing knowing that it might be our last. That was our work: to keep current, to know that life was not guaranteed. Elisabeth was critically ill so many times over the past years that I was always aware of how fragile her time here was. My assumption was this book would be published and she would experience her final work, a bookend to her first work. We always thought of the three books being linked somehow. *On Death and Dying* was her first and the beginning of many. *Life Lessons* was our first book together and we almost called it *On Life and Living*. And then we would do this, her final book, *On Grief and Grieving*.

She did not live to see the book published. A month before she died we spent two days working together. After answering her final questions for this book, she asked me, "Is that all you need? Am I done then?"

"Yes," I told her reluctantly. I never liked it when our work was done, but all the interview tapes were transcribed and I had no more questions. On the previous day, I had gathered the reading material, and on this day, I had just finished reading the final chapters back to her. I knew that from here on, I would only be reading the chapters to her for last-minute changes and proofing.

It was a few minutes before five on our last day of work together, and she asked me to send a message to our editor, Mitchell Ivers, at Scribner, our publishing division at Simon & Schuster. She said into my tape recorder, "Hello, Mitchell. It is 5 P.M. and we are finished. I hope you will enjoy working on this project as much as we have enjoyed writing it. We are done!"

"But Elisabeth," I said, "we're done for today, but we're not done. I'll be reading you the book after it's turned in and after it has been edited for your final approval."

"I am done," she repeated.

Elisabeth always said, "Listen to the dying. They will tell you everything you need to know about when they are dying. And it is easy to miss."

Elisabeth had felt "done" after helping me with my first book, *The Needs of the Dying*, and even said on the cover that it was now " her time to face death." After *Life Lessons*, she said she was done, and yet we were still doing another book.

Elisabeth had said she was ready to die so many times and yet still went on living.

She said, "I know that if I stopped being angry and anxious of my situation and let go, my instincts tell me it would be time for me to die. I am halfway there. My two lessons to learn are patience and learning to receive love. These last nine years have taught me patience, and the weaker and more bed-bound I become, the more I'm learning about receiving love.

"I have nurtured others all my life but rarely let myself be nurtured. I knew when I finally reached this place of acceptance, I could take off and reach another place beyond this life and its limitations. I don't pretend to understand my suffering and I get angry at God about it. I was so mad at God that I have been confined to a chair for nine years that I said, there is a sixth stage—the 'being angry at God stage.' Naturally, being angry with God is just part of the anger stage. It is all part of my own anticipatory grief. I do know that he has a plan. I know that he has a time that will be right for me, and when that time comes I will say yes. And I will then leave my body the same way a cocoon turns into a butterfly. I will experience what I have had the privilege of teaching about for so many years."

I knew intuitively this was going to be her last book, but when she said she was done, I simply thought she was done writing the book, not finished with life. Similarly, I had no idea the grief she invited me to explore and experience was to be a grief over her.

The legendary expert on death and dying, Elisabeth was also the most alive person I've ever met. She liked to be called Elisabeth. To introduce her as Elisabeth Kübler-Ross was far too formal for her. She would refer to herself as a Swiss hillbilly, but this simple, ordinary woman did extraordinary things with her life. In working with the dying, she gave voice to all who could not speak for themselves. She pushed the envelope, not just in learning about the dying but by inviting them to speak and be our teachers.

I remember the first time I was supposed to meet her—in Egypt at an international conference on death and dying. The meeting never happened, because she had a stroke that prevented her from making the trip. Months later, I called to see how she was doing and said, "I hope somehow, someway, our paths will cross."

"How about Tuesday?" she replied.

This was a woman used to making things happen. This was exactly what she needed to do in the beginning of her career in an area of life that no one wanted to explore. Instead of a sterile, isolated death in a far-off hospital corridor, her dream for the dying was a simple, natural death with loved ones around, in a homelike setting—an ordinary death a century earlier.

In the first book we wrote together, *Life Lessons,* there was a chapter on anger. I said to Elisabeth, "We can't have a chapter on anger without you sharing how you feel about being criticized about being so angry when you found out you were dying."

She replied, "People love my stages. They just don't want me to be *in* one." But she was just as human as anyone else.

As she faced her death, she called me and simply said, "Come." For four days, her children, another close friend, Brook, and I sat by her bedside, wondering whether this would truly be the end or if she would surprise us with yet another recovery. As the hours drew into days, we could see that this woman who had written over twenty books on dying was clearly dying herself. For some who idolized her, there was an electric anticipation in the air, that something amazing might happen around her death, that the death and dying expert would have an unsurpassed experience of death.

I don't know what their expectations were, whether it would be music from on high or mysterious rainbows appearing, but none of that happened. Her death did not include any extraordinary measures, for that was not who she was. Elisabeth's death involved instead all the ordinary pleasures that she had so passionately described over the years—her room at home and away from the hospital with lots of flowers, a large picture window, loved ones around, and her grandkids and my kids playing together at the foot of her bed. In the ordinariness of her death, she achieved peace and acceptance, the kind of death that she had first dreamed about for all the dying decades ago.

Elisabeth once said, "Death is but a transition from this life to another existence where there is no more pain or anguish. That knowledge helps me, in my own losses and grief, to know that those I care for are okay. That I will see them again. And those I love now, I will look after when I am gone. I will laugh with them and smile at them. And if they didn't believe in life after death, I will make funny faces at them and say, 'Ha ha, we are here and okay.' I know that the only thing that really lasts forever is love, and I will miss so much about the life I had and the people I have lost."

We miss you too, Elisabeth.

DAVID KESSLER
NOVEMBER 2004

Introduction: Anticipatory Grief

Anticipation heightens the senses and enhances birthdays, holiday celebrations, vacations. Unfortunately, anticipation can also magnify the possibility or reality of a loss. As far as we know, we are the only species aware of the inevitability of our own death. Knowing that we and all of our loved ones will die someday creates anxiety. We see this early on in life.

In childhood we realize at some point that we will die, and not only will we die but those around us will die someday too. That is our beginning of anticipatory grief: fear of the unknown, the pain we will someday experience. It is present in most of our childhood stories and movies as if they were archetypally preparing us.

"Bambi's mother was shot!" many little girls cried to their dads when the movie first came out. That was the moment when many of us in our generation realized someone we cared about could die. For our children, it is Simba's dad dying in *The Lion King*. At an early age we momentarily anticipate that we can lose our parents. In our minds the thought is there, but denial helps us by telling us that it will happen to someone else's parents, Bambi's or Simba's, never our own.

A deeper anticipatory grief occurs years later when someone we love—or we ourselves—have a terminal illness. Anticipatory grief is the "beginning of the end" in our minds. We now operate in two worlds, the safe world that we are used to and the unsafe world in which a loved one might die. We feel that sadness and the unconscious need to prepare our psyche.

Anticipatory grief is generally more silent than grief after a loss. We are often not as verbal. It's a grief we keep to ourselves. We want little active intervention. There is little or no need for words; it is much more a feeling that can be comforted by the touch of a hand or silently sitting together. Most of the time in grief we are focused on the loss in the past, but in anticipatory grief we occupy ourselves with the loss ahead.

When a loved one has to undergo anticipatory grief in order to prepare for the final separation from this world, we have to go through it too. We may not realize it at the time. It may be a strange feeling in the pit of the stomach or an ache in the heart before the loved one dies. We think of the five stages of death occurring for the dying person, but many times loved ones go through them ahead of the death also. This is especially true in long, drawn-out illnesses. Even if you go through any or all of the five stages ahead of the death, you will still go through them again after the loss. Anticipatory grief has its own process; it takes its own time.

Fred and his wife, Karen, had been retired for two years. They had taken a cruise and were enjoying the fruits of their labor. They had one grown son, John, now married. They were a very strong family but also a very stoic one. John's wife would tease him and say, "Does anyone in your family have feelings, or do they just have opinions on events?"

Fred was feeling tired, and a medical workup found he had pancreatic cancer and less than a year to live. The family put together a plan and put all his affairs in order. John's wife told her mother-in-law, "There is heaviness in the air. Why doesn't anyone talk about it?" "We will deal with it when it is time," her mother-in-law replied.

One Sunday, they were having a garage sale. John and his wife were over to help his parents. They'd had garage sales before, but there was noticeably more stuff this time. As Karen and her daughter-in-law were out in front selling, John went inside to see where his dad was. His father was aimlessly walking around the house. John asked, "Dad, are you okay?" His father replied, "I am not sure what to do."

John felt sadness underneath and wanted to help his father. "Come outside and help," he said. As they passed through the garage, his father stopped and looked at his workbench. His father had loved working in the garage fixing things. John and his father had recently had a talk about how John doesn't really fix things like his dad and how the world has changed. "Things are so inexpensive and time so valuable," John had said, "you don't fix it, you buy a new one."

Before leaving the garage, Fred stopped and surveyed his tools. John watched his father, wondering what was going on inside him. Fred then turned to John and said, "Will you bring all these tools out front to the garage sale?"

John said, "Dad, are you sure?"

"Yes," he said and walked outside.

John began gathering the tools from the bench, the walls, and the drawers. He could picture each tool in his father's hand when he was a child watching his father work away. John began feeling sad, and before long he was standing in the garage alone, sobbing.

His father walked in and put his arm around him and said, "For all of us, son. For all of us."

Even the most stoic family is not immune to anticipatory grief. John was the son who expressed the feelings held within them all. He was demonstrating that we grieve after someone dies but we also grieve before.

Anticipating a loss is an important part of experiencing that loss. We often think of it as part of the process our loved ones go through as they face their own death themselves. Yet for those who will survive the loss of a loved one, it is the beginning of the grieving process. Such anticipation may help us brace ourselves for what is to come, but we should be aware that the anticipation of an event may be just as powerful as the event itself.

Forewarned is not always forearmed. Experiencing anticipatory grief may or may not make the grieving process easier or shorten it. It may bring only feelings of guilt that we were grieving before the loss actually occurred. We may experience all five stages of loss (denial, anger, bargaining, depression, and acceptance) before the actual death. We may experience only anger and denial. Not everyone experiences anticipatory grief, and if they do, certainly not in the same way.

We may also experience the limbo of loss in anticipatory grief, those times when our loved one is not getting better and not dying yet, but in a state of poor health with little quality of life. For those dying, it may be a time of quiet desperation or outright anger: those moments when our loved one can watch TV but is not able to change the channel, or they are hungry but unable to hold a spoon.

Loved ones witness and feel all those moments also at their own level. One person described the time in between as "not worse than death, but death or worse," and their loved one was stuck in "worse." The limbo of loss is in itself a loss to be mourned. Uncertainty can be an excruciating existence. It is the loss of life, going nowhere or going nowhere slowly without knowing if there will be a loss.

In cases with years to prepare for a death, we may not experience the stages after death. In long-term diseases like ALS, MS, or Alzheimers disease, we may be losing our loved ones so gradually that there is time to experience all five stages over a period of years.

In some cases, anticipatory grief may happen months or years before the loss. It is important for us to remember that this anticipatory grief stands alone from the grief we feel after a loss. For many, anticipatory grief is just a prelude to the painful process we face, a double grief that will ultimately bring healing.

1. The Five Stages of Grief

Denial, Anger, Bargaining, Depression,
and Acceptance

The stages have evolved since their introduction, and they have been very misunderstood over the past three decades. They were never meant to help tuck messy emotions into neat packages. They are responses to loss that many people have, but there is not a typical response to loss, as there is no typical loss. Our grief is as individual as our lives.

The five stages—denial, anger, bargaining, depression, and acceptance—are a part of the framework that makes up our learning to live with the one we lost. They are tools to help us frame and identify what we may be feeling. But they are not stops on some linear timeline in grief. Not everyone goes through all of them or goes in a prescribed order.

Our hope is that with these stages comes the knowledge of grief's terrain, making us better equipped to cope with life and loss.

DENIAL

Denial in grief has been misinterpreted over the years. When the stage of denial was first introduced in *On Death and Dying*, it focused on the person who was dying. In this book, *On Grief and Grieving*, the person who may be in denial is grieving the loss of a loved one. In a person who is dying, denial may look like disbelief. They may be going about life and actually denying that a terminal illness exists. For a person who has lost a loved one, however, the denial is more symbolic than literal.

This does not mean that you literally don't know your loved one has died. It means you come home and you can't believe that your wife isn't going to walk in the door at any minute or that your husband isn't just away on a business trip. You simply can't fathom that he will never walk through that door again.

When we are in denial, we may respond at first by being paralyzed with shock or blanketed with numbness. The denial is still not *denial of the actual death*, even though someone may be saying, "I can't believe he's dead." The person is actually saying that, at first, because it is too much for his or her psyche.

Alicia was accustomed to Matthew's being away on business trips. His work required him to travel the world, and Alicia had accompanied him on several trips that took him to places she wanted to see. She also witnessed the jet lag, hectic schedule, time changes, and delayed flights.

On his current trip, Alicia was surprised that he'd been scheduled to arrive in Delhi and he hadn't phoned her yet. After two days, he called and apologized, explaining that there were phone problems in his hotel. She understood because this often happened when he traveled to third world countries.

The next call came two days later in the middle of the night from one of her husband's coworkers. He gently told her that he had very bad news. Matthew had been killed in a car accident. He said there were very few details as yet but the home office would be contacting her.

Alicia couldn't believe her ears. After she hung up the phone she immediately thought, "Did I just dream that? This must be a mistake." She called her sister, who arrived just as the sun was rising. They waited until eight o'clock and called the home office only to find out they didn't know of any problem, much less a tragedy like this. But they said they would look into it immediately. For the rest of the morning Alicia couldn't stop wondering if she had dreamed the phone call. Was there a mistake? The next call came at noon, confirming that indeed, last night's bad news was true.

For the next few days Alicia made funeral arrangements, all the while saying, "This can't be true. I know when the body arrives it won't be him." The night before the funeral, Alicia finally saw her dear husband's body. She looked at his face to make sure it wasn't just someone who looked like Matthew, but when she saw his wedding ring, there was no more question.

During the weeks after the funeral, she would call friends and family and say, "I keep thinking he's still on the trip and he just can't get to a phone. I know he's out there somewhere trying to get home." She would usually end up crying over the reality that he was not coming home.

Alicia's story clearly illustrates how denial works. At times she thought it might be a dream, but she did the appropriate thing by calling her sister about the loss. The reality sank in even more when she saw the body and the ring on his finger. It would be easy to say that she was in denial because she kept thinking Matthew's death was not real. It would be equally easy to say she was not in denial because she kept going through with funeral arrangements. But both are true. She couldn't believe it *and* her mind could not fully process it. Denial helped her to unconsciously manage her feelings. Even after the funeral, she often thought he still might just be on a trip. This was still denial working very subtly, to give her moments away from her pain.

This first stage of grieving helps us to survive the loss. In this stage, the world becomes meaningless and overwhelming. Life makes no sense. We are in a state of shock and denial. We go numb. We wonder how we can go on, if we can go on, why we should go on. We try to find a way to simply get through each day. Denial and shock help us to cope and make survival possible. Denial helps us to pace our feelings of grief. There is a grace in denial. It is nature's way of letting in only as much as we can handle.

These feelings are important; they are the psyche's protective mechanisms. Letting in all the feelings associated with loss at once would be overwhelming emotionally. We can't believe what has happened because we actually *can't* believe what has happened. To fully believe at this stage would be too much.

The denial often comes in the form of our questioning our reality: Is it true? Did it really happen? Are they really gone? Think about the idea that you can't get over someone. It is more that you learn to live with the loss and not forget the person.

People often find themselves telling the story of their loss over and over, which is one way that our mind deals with trauma. It is a way of denying the pain while trying to accept the reality of the loss. As denial fades, it is slowly replaced with the reality of the loss.

You begin to question the how and why. How did this happen? you may ask, as you review the circumstances. You are no longer in an external story-telling mode; now you turn inward as you begin the search for understanding. You explore the circumstances surrounding the loss. Did it have to happen? Did it have to happen that way? Could anything have prevented it?

The finality of the loss begins to gradually sink in. She is not coming back. This time he didn't make it. With each question asked, you begin to believe they are really gone.

As you accept the reality of the loss and start to ask yourself questions, you are unknowingly beginning the healing process. You are becoming stronger, and the denial is beginning to fade. But as you proceed, all the feelings you were denying begin to surface.

ANGER

This stage presents itself in many ways: anger at your loved one that he didn't take better care of himself or anger that you didn't take better care of him. Anger does not have to be logical or valid. You may be angry that you didn't see this coming and when you did, nothing could stop it. You may be angry with the doctors for not being able to save someone so dear to you. You may be angry that bad things could happen to someone who meant so much to you.

You may also be angry that you're left behind and you should have had more time together. You know intellectually that your loved one didn't want to die. But emotionally, all you know is that he *did* die. It was not supposed to happen, or at least not now.

It is important to remember that the anger surfaces once you are feeling safe enough to know you will probably survive whatever comes. At first, the fact that you lived through the loss is surprising to you. Then more feelings hit, and anger is usually at the front of the line as feelings of sadness, panic, hurt, and loneliness also appear, stronger than ever. Loved ones and friends are often taken aback by these feelings, because they surface just as you were beginning to function at a basic level again.

You may also be angry with yourself that you couldn't *stop* it from happening. Not that you had the power, but you had the will. The will to save a life is not the power to stop a death. But most of all, you may be angry at this unexpected, undeserved, and unwanted situation in which you find yourself. Someone once shared, "I'm angry that I have to keep living in a world where I can't find her, call her, or see her. I can't find the person I loved or needed anywhere. She is not really where her body is now. The heavenly bodies elude me. The all-ness or one-ness of her spiritual existence escapes me. I am lost and full of rage."

Anger is a necessary stage of the healing process. Be willing to feel your anger, even though it may seem endless. The more you truly feel it, the more it will begin to dissipate and the more you will heal. There are many other emotions under the anger and you will get to them in time, but anger is the emotion we are most used to managing. We often choose it to avoid the feelings underneath until we are ready to face them. It may feel all-consuming, but as long as it doesn't consume you for a long period of time, it is part of your emotional management. It is a useful emotion until you've moved past the first waves of it. Then you will be ready to go deeper. In the process of grief and grieving you will have many subsequent visits with anger in its many forms.

When Jan's husband died, all her married friends overwhelmed her with advice on how to get through it. But the women who shared loving tips of guidance had not lost their husbands. Jan would listen politely but think, "What do *you* know? Your husband is still alive."

Jan loved her friends and knew they meant well. She said, "The only thing that stops me from letting them 'really have it' is that I know they will understand someday too, and I know they will understand hurt better."

The truth is that anger has no limits. It can extend not only to your friends, the doctors, your family, yourself, and your loved one who died, but also to God. You may ask, "Where is God in this? Where is his love? His powerfulness? His compassion? Is this really God's will?" You may not want people to talk to you about God's plan or his mysteries. You may feel like saying, "God, my husband has died. Was this your plan?" Or "I don't want any mysteries, I just want him back. My faith feels rocked and destroyed." "I feel not given to but taken from." "God is a disappointment, and my faith feels shattered with his plan for me and my loved one."

Maybe you are angry that God didn't take better care of your loved one. It's as if you hope that in your case, God will realize some huge mistake has been made and your loved one will be returned to you. There you sit, alone with your anger, wondering how to reconcile your spirituality and your religion with this loss and anger. You may not even be interested in reconciliation. Many don't dare talk about these feelings. You think, maybe God is mad at me and this is what I get for being mad at him. Perhaps when our loved one was dying and we already experienced the bargaining stage, we asked God to intervene and save our loved one. Now after the loved one has died, we are left with a God who, in our eyes, did not come to our aid when we needed him the most.

We often assume that if we are good people we will not suffer the ills of the world. You may feel that you and your loved one honored your part of the deal: You went to church, synagogue, or your particular place of worship. You were loving, kind, and charitable. You did all the things you were told. You believed you would be rewarded if you did. Well, this loss is no reward. We also assume that if we care for our bodies, eat right, get medical checkups, and exercise, we will be granted good health. These assumptions come crashing down around us when the good, the just, the loving, the healthy, the young, and even the needed and most wanted die on us.

When Heather's teenage daughter died at sixteen, Heather was furious at God for allowing her to die so young, with a life so unlived. Heather's family were deeply involved in the church that had been a strong support during her daughter's illnesses, but they had difficulty dealing with Heather's anger. She no longer wanted to hear about the God who answers prayers, since her prayers had not been answered. She felt judged by her friends at church for having so much anger at God.

A friend said to her cautiously, "Be careful not to evoke the wrath of God."

At that, Heather was even more enraged. "What is he going to do," she retorted, "take my daughter away? What's he going to do, take me? That would be fine. I'd rather be with her than be here."

Her friend knelt down and said tenderly, "Let's pray for forgiveness."

At that moment Heather decided to leave behind her church and a number of friends. It was years before she walked back into the church.

If we ask people to move through their anger too fast, we only alienate them. Whenever we ask people to be different than they are, or to feel something different, we are not accepting them as they are and where they are. Nobody likes to be asked to change and not be accepted as they are. We like it even less in the midst of grief.

Today, most churches and clergy understand it is not unusual for people to feel anger toward God. Many churches have started bereavement groups in which priests and ministers encourage expression of all feelings. They allow it and are not put off if you speak of it. Consider talking to your church, temple, or place of worship about it.

People often wonder about their God and his role. One member of the clergy shared that he expects members of the congregation to question their relationship with God after a loss. He said that one of his goals is to help grieving members. He said, "Sometimes we do a wonderful job with rituals immediately after death, but I want my congregation to help those in grief with the day-to-day feelings of loss also. Once you allow yourself to feel and speak out the anger, you may find that your God is strong enough to handle your anger, strong enough to feel compassion and love for you, even in the midst of your anger at him."

Underneath anger is pain, *your* pain. It is natural to feel deserted and abandoned, but we live in a society that fears anger. People often tell us our anger is misplaced, inappropriate, or disproportionate. Some people may feel your anger is harsh or too much. It is their problem if they don't know how to deal with it. Unfortunately for them, they too will know the anger of loss someday. But for now, your job is to honor your anger by allowing yourself to be angry. Scream if you need to. Find a solitary place and let it out.

Anger is strength and it can be an anchor, giving temporary structure to the nothingness of loss. At first grief feels like being lost at sea: no connection to anything. Then you get angry at someone, maybe a person who didn't attend the funeral, maybe a person who isn't around, maybe a person who is different now that your loved one has died. Suddenly you have a structure— your anger toward them. The anger becomes a bridge over the open sea, a connection from you to them. It is something to hold on to, and a connection made from the strength of anger feels better than nothing.

We usually know more about suppressing anger than feeling it. Tell a counselor how angry you are. Share it with friends and family. Scream into a pillow. Find ways to get it out without hurting yourself or someone else. Try walking, swimming, gardening—any type of exercise helps you externalize your anger. Do not bottle up anger inside. Instead, explore it. The anger is just another indication of the intensity of your love.

Anger means you are progressing, that you are allowing all those feelings that were simply too much before to come to the surface. It is important to feel the anger without judging it, without attempting to find meaning in it. It may take many forms: anger at the health-care system, at life, at your loved one for leaving. Life is unfair. Death is unfair. Anger is a natural reaction to the unfairness of loss. Unfortunately, however, anger can isolate you from friends and family at the precise time you may need them the most.

You also may experience feelings of guilt, which is anger turned inward on yourself. But you are not to blame. If you could change things, you would, but you can't. Anger affirms that you *can* feel, that you *did* love, and that you *have* lost.

The more anger you allow, the more feelings you will find underneath. Anger is the most immediate emotion, but as you deal with it, you will find other feelings hidden. Mostly you will find the pain of loss. The power of your anger may overwhelm you because for some it may be in proportion to the amount of lost love that it represents. It may seem that if you go into the pain, you will never come out of it or that the pain will never end. You *will* come out the other end. The anger will subside, and the feelings of loss will change form again.

Don't let anyone diminish the importance of feeling your anger fully. And don't let anyone criticize your anger, not even you.

BARGAINING

Before a loss, it seems you will do anything if only your loved one may be spared. "Please, God," you bargain, "I will never be angry at my wife again if you'll just let her live." After a loss, bargaining may take the form of a temporary truce. "What if I devote the rest of my life to helping others? Then can I wake up and realize this has all been a bad dream?"

We become lost in a maze of "if only . . ." or "What if . . ." statements. We want life returned to what it was; we want our loved one restored. We want to go back in time: find the tumor sooner, recognize the illness more quickly, stop the accident from happening . . . if only, if only, if only.

Guilt is often bargaining's companion. The "if onlys" cause us to find fault with ourselves and what we "think" we could have done differently. We may even bargain with the pain. We will do anything not to feel the pain of this loss. We remain in the past, trying to negotiate our way out of the hurt.

As Howard turned seventy-five, he was determined to keep himself and his sixty-six-year-old wife, Millie, in good health. He had read somewhere that walking every day would keep them fit, possibly ward off Alzheimers, and help them sleep better. Millie knew it was easier to go along with the program than to resist.

On the sixth day, after they returned from a busy morning of errands, Howard got ready for their walk. Millie looked at Howard and said, "Do we have to do this every day? A day off won't hurt."

Howard lectured, "It takes thirty days to create a habit. We have to do this every day, no matter what."

Millie rolled her eyes and said, "Can we at least wait until later? We just got in."

He grabbed her sweater. "Let's just get this over with. You'll be happy when it's done."

They walked a block and stepped into the crosswalk. When they were halfway across the street a car came barreling around the corner and struck them, Millie first, then Howard. In a moment, a disoriented Howard looked up and saw Millie lying on the pavement a few feet away. Suddenly someone was asking him if he was okay. He responded, "My wife!" The paramedics assured him that they were taking care of her.

At the hospital Howard was treated for numerous bruises and a broken arm. Millie was not so fortunate. She had sustained massive internal injuries and was taken to surgery.

Howard sat, surrounded by family, repeating over and over in his mind, "Please, God, let her live—I'll never make Millie do anything she doesn't want to do . . . I'll be a better person . . . you'll see, I'll volunteer, I'll devote my life to you . . . please, not now."

The surgeon walked in an hour later and said, "I'm sorry, we couldn't save her."

People often think of the stages as lasting weeks or months. They forget that the stages are responses to feelings that can last for minutes or hours as we flip in and out of one and then another. We do not enter and leave each individual stage in a linear fashion. We may feel one, then another, and back again to the first one.

For Howard, his first days alone were a bag of mixed emotions. "She can't be gone," he'd say. Then he'd feel rage when he learned the car that hit his wife was in the process of being stolen. At bedtime, he'd bargain again. "Please, God, let me fall asleep and wake up realizing this was all a dream. I will do anything to have her back."

For the next few minutes he'd run a fantasy of waking up with Millie next to him. He tells her about the horrible nightmare he had. Over breakfast they laugh as he promises from now on they will walk only if they both really want to.

His thoughts were bargaining with all the what ifs . . . "What if I had said, 'Sure, we can walk later'? What if I had never read the article on walking?"

His family would have to remind him that he wasn't responsible for the accident. "You were trying to keep her healthy," they'd say, "not leading her to her death. You had no way of knowing that some reckless driver in a stolen car was about to come flying around the corner." They thought of his reaction as one of guilt.

He would tell them that he knew it wasn't his fault. Bargaining for him was his escape from the pain, a distraction from the sad reality of his life without her.

In his first six months, denial, anger, and a lot of bargaining were his constant companions. They would eventually lead him to depression, still mixed with the "if onlys" of bargaining. Acceptance came in bits and pieces over the next few years.

For Howard, bargaining was a key stage, since he was still holding a piece of the alternate future in which his wife's death never happened. Bargaining can be an important reprieve from pain that occupies one's grief. He never believed the bargaining; he just found relief in it momentarily.

In other cases, bargaining can help our mind move from one state of loss to another. It can be a way station that gives our psyche the time it may need to adjust. Bargaining may fill the gaps that our strong emotions generally dominate, which often keep suffering at a distance. It allows us to believe that we can restore order to the chaos that has taken over. Bargaining changes over time. We may start out bargaining for our loved one to be saved. Later, we may even bargain that we might die instead of our loved one.

When we accept that they are going to die we may bargain that their death will be painless. After a death, bargaining often moves from the past to the future. We may bargain that we will see our loved ones again in heaven. We may bargain and ask for a respite from illnesses in our family, or that no other tragedies visit our loved ones. A mother who loses a child may bargain that her other children remain safe and healthy.

In his well-known song "Tears in Heaven," Eric Clapton writes about his young son who fell tragically to his death. Some of the lyrics could be interpreted as the bargaining stage, when he wonders if he will stop crying once he finally gets to heaven.

As we move through the bargaining process, the mind alters past events while exploring all those "what if" and "if only" statements. Sadly, the mind inevitably comes to the same conclusion . . . the tragic reality is that our loved one is truly gone.

DEPRESSION

After bargaining, our attention moves squarely into the present. Empty feelings present themselves, and grief enters our lives on a deeper level, deeper than we ever imagined. This depressive stage feels as though it will last forever. It's important to understand that this depression is not a sign of mental illness. It is the appropriate response to a great loss. We withdraw from life, left in a fog of intense sadness, wondering, perhaps, if there is any point in going on alone. Why go on at all?

Morning comes, but you don't care. A voice in your head says it is time to get out of bed, but you have no desire to do so. You may not even have a reason. Life feels pointless. To get out of bed may as well be climbing a mountain. You feel heavy, and being upright takes something from you that you just don't have to give.

If you find a way to get through your daily activities, each of them seems as empty and pointless as the last one. Why eat? Or why stop eating? You don't care enough to care. If you could care about what was going on, it might scare you, so you don't want to care about anything.

Others around you see this lethargy and want to get you out of your "depression."

Depression after a loss is too often seen as unnatural: a state to be fixed, something to snap out of. The first question to ask yourself is whether the situation you're in is actually depressing. The loss of a loved one is a very depressing situation, and depression is a normal and appropriate response. To *not* experience depression after a loved one dies would be unusual. When a loss fully settles in your soul, the realization that your loved one didn't get better this time and is not coming back is understandably depressing.

When we are grieving, people may wonder about us, and we may wonder about ourselves. The heavy, dark feelings of depression that come with grief, however normal, are often seen in our society as something to be treated. Of course clinical depression, untreated, can lead to a worsening of one's mental state. But in grief, depression is a way for nature to keep us protected by shutting down the nervous system so that we can adapt to something we feel we cannot handle.

If grief is a process of healing, then depression is one of the many necessary steps along the way. If you have the awareness

21

to recognize you are in depression or have been told by multiple friends you are depressed, your first response may be to resist and look for a way out. Seeking a way out of depression feels like going into a hurricane and sailing around the inside perimeter, fearful that there is no exit door.

As tough as it is, depression can be dealt with in a paradoxical way. See it as a visitor, perhaps an unwelcome one, but one who is visiting whether you like it or not. Make a place for your guest. Invite your depression to pull up a chair with you in front of the fire, and sit with it, without looking for a way to escape. Allow the sadness and emptiness to cleanse you and help you explore your loss in its entirety. When you allow yourself to experience depression, it will leave as soon as it has served its purpose in your loss. As you grow stronger, it may return from time to time, but that is how grief works.

A smart, charismatic woman, Claudia was surprised at the depth of her depression when her grown daughter was dying. She thought that was as depressing as it would get, but after her daughter died, the depression returned. "It was different than when my daughter was alive," Claudia said. "When she was fighting for her life, my depression had walls, a structure within which fights had to be fought. But after she died, the depression that returned felt like being hit with a punching bag. I was knocked down over and over, with no desire to get up again."

Claudia reported that her depression eventually passed and she began to do more and get out more. She went back to work part-time and started accepting offers from friends to do things. "Time had passed; I was better, functional and improving, when suddenly the depression returned. I'd thought I was done with it, but I guess it wasn't done with me.

"This time, I heard a loud voice, literally heralding the reality that my daughter was never coming back. This time the depression had no walls, ceiling, or floor. It felt even more endless than before and, once again, I had to deal with this old familiar guest. I learned the only way around this storm was through it."

The stages of loss—denial, anger, bargaining, depression, and acceptance—have been widely used and misused. Our society almost seems to be involved in a "stamp out depression" campaign. Sometimes intervention is vital, but most of the time, we do not allow the normal depression that comes with grief to have its place.

Clinical depression is a group of illnesses that may be characterized by a long-term or excessively depressed state. But our society often considers an appropriate sadness to be depression requiring fixing. Normal depression is the sadness we feel at certain times in our lives, the common cold of mental illnesses. We even have television advertisements offering help with it, selling pills promising to get rid of it. When a normal depression becomes a clinical depression requiring professional help, antidepressants may be helpful for a time.

When depression follows loss, there are specific sorrows that can be identified. In more serious and long-lasting depressions, it is difficult to receive support. In this case antidepressant medications may be useful, to help lift someone out of what seems to be a bottomless depression. Only a trained medical professional familiar with the griever's situation can make an accurate diagnosis.

Treating depression is a balancing act. We must accept sadness as an appropriate, natural stage of loss without letting an unmanaged, ongoing depression leech our quality of life. The use of antidepressants remains a controversial topic, especially when a loss is involved. Some people are worried that if they take antidepressants, they will miss the process of grief. If only that were so.

The reality is that your grief is there and available for processing, on or off medication. Some people feel that medications simply put a floor in for them to deal with their depression. In some cases, depression may need to be managed by using a combination of support, psychotherapy, and antidepressant medications.

As difficult as it is to endure, depression has elements that can be helpful in grief. It slows us down and allows us to take real stock of the loss. It makes us rebuild ourselves from the ground up. It clears the deck for growth. It takes us to a deeper place in our soul that we would not normally explore.

Most people's initial reaction to sad people is to try to cheer them up, to tell them not to look at things so grimly, to look at the bright side of life. This cheering-up reaction is often an expression of that person's own needs and that person's own inability to tolerate a long face over an extended period. A mourner should be allowed to experience his sorrow, and he will be grateful for those who can sit with him without telling him not to be sad. A mourner may be in the midst of life and yet not a participant in all the activities considered living: unable to get out of bed; tense, irritable, unable to concentrate; unable to care about anything. No matter what our surroundings may hold, we feel alone. This is what hitting the bottom feels like. You wonder if you will ever feel anything again or if this is what life will be like forever.

ACCEPTANCE

Acceptance is often confused with the notion of being all right or okay with what has happened. This is not the case. Most people don't ever feel okay or all right about the loss of a loved one. This stage is about accepting the reality that our loved one is physically gone and recognizing that this new reality is the permanent reality. We will never like this reality or make it okay, but eventually we accept it. We learn to live with it. It is the new norm with which we must learn to live. This is where our final healing and adjustment can take a firm hold, despite the fact that healing often looks and feels like an unattainable state.

Healing looks like remembering, recollecting, and reorganizing. We may cease to be angry with God; we may become aware of the commonsense reasons for our loss, even if we never actually understand the reasons. We the survivors begin to realize sadly that it was our loved one's time to die. Of course it was too soon for us, and probably too soon for him or her, too. Perhaps he was very old or full of pain and disease. Perhaps her body was worn down and she was ready for her journey to be over. But *our* journey still continues. It is not yet time for us to die; in fact, it is time for us to heal.

We must try to live now in a world where our loved one is missing. In resisting this new norm, at first we may want to maintain life as it was before a loved one died. In time, through bits and pieces of acceptance, however, we see that we cannot maintain the past intact. It has been forever changed and we must readjust. We must learn to reorganize roles, reassign them to others or take them on ourselves. The more of your identity that was connected to your loved one, the harder it will be to do this.

As we heal, we learn who we are and who our loved one was in life. In a strange way, as we move through grief, healing brings us closer to the person we loved. A new relationship begins. We learn to live with the loved one we lost. We start the process of reintegration, trying to put back the pieces that have been ripped away.

Alan, seventeen years old, was thrilled to go to the basketball championship that was being held downtown in the sports arena. After the game, in the parking lot, Alan walked ten feet to his car and was randomly shot and killed by a gang member.

His father, Keith, and his mother, Donna, could not understand why their son was killed. They were filled with anger as they spent their days and nights trying to raise their other two kids, go to work, and follow the all-consuming ongoing investigation into the killing.

A close couple, friends of Keith and Donna's, became concerned because they were not available to get together for meals or anything else. One evening the couple dropped in out of concern and said to Keith and Donna, "You have to accept this loss. Your son is gone and none of this is going to bring him back. Haven't you heard about the five stages? You've done all the others. All you need now is acceptance."

Keith got angry with his friend and asked, "What part of Alan's death don't you think I accept? At his grave today, I cried like a baby. If I didn't accept it, would I go to his grave? We're not setting a place for him at the dinner table tonight. We live in reality, his room is empty every night. How much more acceptance can we feel?"

The friend looked down and said, "I just hate to see you in so much pain."

Keith replied, "Believe me, I hate to be in so much pain."

We have found that is it not unusual for people like Keith and Donna's friends to misunderstand the stages. Acceptance is not about liking a situation. It is about acknowledging all that has been lost and learning to live with that loss. It would be too soon for Keith to be able to accept this situation. He can acknowledge the reality of the loss, but it would be unrealistic to think he should have found some peace with it by then.

After closing arguments in the murder case, it took the jury only five hours to come back with a guilty verdict. The gang member who killed Alan was sentenced to life in prison, and Keith and Donna went back to their own lives.

Keith actually had a new loss to deal with, which was the emptiness he now felt without the trial to consume his time. It made the absence of his son's loss even louder.

We think it is important for people to understand that gradually, in your own time, you can begin to find some peace with what has happened. In situations such as murder, it is vital to understand we have a legal system, not necessarily a justice system. For some, the only justice would be to have their loved one back. Acceptance is a process that we experience, not a final stage with an end point.

For Keith, no one else could know how much acceptance he was capable of or how time would affect his process. After five years Keith felt he had found as much acceptance as was possible. Then he was notified that the shooter was up for his first parole hearing. Keith felt all his hard-earned acceptance drain out of him. By the time of the hearing he was once again filled with anger. The proceedings were brief and parole was denied. Keith was struck by how quickly it happened and by the tears of the shooter's father. For the first time, Keith realized there were victims on both ends of the gun.

Keith walked over to him and shook his hand. At that moment, something happened for Keith as his anger was replaced by a curiosity. He wanted to know what this other father's life was like and what led him to this same place. Over the next few years the two men formed an alliance to help gang members stop the violence and find their place in the world. They went from school to school in the inner city with their story.

Keith's acceptance was a journey that was deeper than he ever expected. And it happened over many years, not many months or days. Not everyone will or can fully embrace those who have hurt us, as Keith did, but there is always a struggle that leads us to our own personal and unique acceptance.

Keith's story is just one example of how, little by little, we withdraw our energy from the loss and begin to invest it in life. We put the loss into perspective, learning how to remember our loved ones and commemorate the loss. We start to form new relationships or put more time into old ones.

Finding acceptance may be just having more good days than bad. As we begin to live again and enjoy our life, we often feel that in doing so, we are betraying our loved one. We can never replace what has been lost, but we can make new connections, new meaningful relationships, new interdependencies. Instead of denying our feelings, we listen to our needs; we move, we change, we grow, we evolve. We may start to reach out to others and become involved in their lives. We invest in our friendships and in our relationship with ourself. We begin to live again, but we cannot do so until we have given grief its time.

2. The Inner World of Grief

YOUR LOSS

An unimaginable, indescribable loss has taken place. It has inflicted a wound so deep that numbness and excruciating pain are the material of which it is made.

Everyone experiences many losses throughout life, but the death of a loved one is unmatched for its emptiness and profound sadness. Your world stops. You know the exact time your loved one died—or the exact moment you were told. It is marked in your mind. Your world takes on a slowness, a surrealness. It seems strange that the clocks in the world continue when your inner clock does not.

Your life continues, but you are not sure why. A different life appears before you, one in which your loved one will no longer be physically present. No one can give you words to make you feel better; there are none. You will survive, though you may not be sure how or even if you want to.

Your loss and the grief that accompanies it are very personal, different from anyone else's. Others may share the experience of their losses. They may try to console you in the only way they know. But your loss stands alone in its meaning to you, in its painful uniqueness.

*　　*　　*

Brian, in his late fifties, had to have his leg amputated. It was a terrible loss. During rehabilitation sessions he saw another man who had had both legs amputated, and now he thought less of his loss and felt unjustified in feeling bad. He said he suddenly realized there were people worse off than he was. The next day in his rehabilitation session he saw a young man with both legs who just needed a cane, and then he felt his loss more keenly. The two men had a chance to talk after their session about what had brought them to this point. Brian shared that he had lost his leg because of diabetes. The man with a cane told of the car accident that had caused a minor injury to his back and said he needed to regain his strength. Brian, still comparing losses, said, "Well, at least you have two legs." The man with the cane said, "Yes I do, but I lost my wife in the accident."

When you compare losses, someone else's may seem greater or lesser than your own, but all losses are painful. If you lost a husband at seventy, there will be someone who lost a husband at forty-eight. If you lost a parent at twelve, there will be someone who lost their parent at five years old—or at fifteen years. Losses are *very personal* and comparisons never apply. No loss counts more than another. It is your loss that counts for you. It is your loss that affects you. Your loss is deep and deserves your personal attention without comparison. You are the only one who can survey the magnitude of your loss. No one will ever know the meaning of what was shared, the deepness of the void that shadows your future. You alone know your loss. Only you can fully appreciate the depth of the physical relationship that has ended.

We all play many roles in our lives: spouse, parent, child, family member, friend. You knew your loved one in a way that no one else ever did or ever will. One person's dying touches many people in many different ways; everyone feels that loss individually. Your task in your own mourning and grieving is to fully recognize your own loss, to see it as only you can. In paying the respect and taking the time it deserves, you bring integrity to the deep loss that is yours.

RELIEF

For many, a strange and unexpected feeling sits amid the loss: a feeling of relief that contrasts with the pervading sadness. It feels out of place, out of step, and is often considered wrong. Why would you feel a sense of relief at the loss of someone so close and so dear?

If you feel relief, it may be because your loved one was suffering and you are grateful it has ended. Watching or even thinking about a loved one's suffering places a heavy pain on top of the sadness. Of course you wanted her to live long, fully, and well. But that was not an option.

It is her endless suffering you wanted to end, which is why you feel somewhat relieved that she is dead. Hence the confusion: the relief and sadness mix together in a situation that has no resolve. When this occurs, your relief is the recognition that the suffering has ended, the pain is over, the disease no longer lives. Your loved one no longer has that illness, that disease. It has stopped causing her pain.

Your relief may be in proportion to the amount and length of suffering. For example, when President Ronald Reagan died from Alzheimers disease, he had been suffering for close to a decade. Nancy, his wife, was deeply saddened and allowed her loss to be viewed by the world. Many people, including some family members, talked about the relief they felt now that his suffering was over. He had seen so many years of pain with no quality of life, and all they could do was watch him decline. At the end of that, anyone would be relieved.

For those who did not experience a long, drawn-out death, however, the task of separating the relief from the loss becomes even more difficult. There is the relief of knowing your loved one is no longer suffering. There is the reality that neither are you. Suffering is a family affair, and everyone endures it together.

One day, John went into the hospital for a simple cardiac procedure. He and his wife, Amanda, were informed, just like everyone else, that something could go wrong. They accepted that, and he turned out to be the one in a thousand who suffered complications. Before Amanda knew what was going on, John was diagnosed with Acute Respiratory Distress Syndrome (ARDS), which is an inflammatory process that results in moderate to severe loss of lung function. She could not believe that this illness existed and that his body was suddenly overcome with respiratory failure and massive infection. The odds were so against this happening. He needed to be resuscitated not once but twice, his temperature reached 107 degrees, and a few days after the surgery he lay in the ICU with little brain function and even less hope for survival.

For the next ten days his wife watched his face covered in tape that held in tubes so that a machine could breathe for him. On the tenth day, he had his final cardiac arrest and did not survive. Amanda was stunned. Just two weeks prior, he had appeared and felt absolutely fine. But she also felt relief that he was not suffering after ten seemingly interminable days.

Her task was to integrate the sadness with the relief, a classic example of mixed emotions. Most of us have experienced mixed emotions in our lives. We think we should have only one emotion, but many conflicting emotions exist in us at the same time. Amanda was right to feel the sorrow and the relief, but how could she give each of these emotions its due?

In grief we often have a deep well of different emotions occurring at the same time, which is what makes grief confusing. We don't have to choose which emotion is right or wrong. We can feel each emotion as it occurs and understand that relief is not disloyalty but rather a sign of deep love. Even as you are an unwilling character in your loss, you know that your loss will be easier for you to bear than the suffering was for your loved one. That is real love.

Relief plays out in many ways: it may occur for you when you finally get all the medical equipment out of the house. But while you transform the room from a makeshift hospital room to a bedroom once again, the subsequent emptiness will create a new pain. The day you go back to work may feel like a guilty pleasure, as you feel the relief of returning to your work life as you knew it before the tragedy. But then 4:30 P.M. hits and you realize you will be going home to an empty house. Even when you are happy to see your friends again and laugh at their jokes, the relief is mixed with sadness and, maybe, guilt.

It is important to understand that it is not unusual to feel relief, even in the midst of the sadness. This is a normal reaction and not a reason to feel guilty. The relief you feel is the calm *after* the storm.

EMOTIONAL REST

We are not accustomed to the emotional upheaval that accompanies a loss. People experience a wide array of emotions after a loss, from not caring to being on edge to feeling angry or sad about everything. We can go from feeling okay to feeling devastated in a minute without warning. We can have mood swings that are hard for anyone around us to comprehend, because even we don't understand them. One minute we are okay. The next we're in tears. This is how grief works.

We can touch the pain directly for only so long until we have to back away. We think about our work, get momentarily distracted in something else, process the feelings, and go for more. If we did not go back and forth emotionally, we could never have the strength to find peace in our loss.

Vanessa was returning to the work world a few months after her son died in a car accident. She had been an office manager for years, and when someone offered her the same kind of job, it made sense to take a position doing the same line of work. But very soon, multitasking became multiemotional and multidemanding. After a few days on the job, she knew she had made a mistake, that this kind of work was more than she was prepared to handle.

"I'm so sorry," she said. "I shouldn't have taken this job. It is more than I am capable of right now. This is a perfect job for me in about a year, but right now, I need simple work like being a receptionist with a phone and a list of numbers." Vanessa knew her emotional limits and was brave enough to put her emotional well-being first.

The other extreme would be complete denial with no hope for ever returning to life. That would place us in a constant emotional reenactment of our loss with no chance for learning to live with it in a healthy way. We would see loss and feel it everywhere. The smallest loss would produce the biggest overreactions.

Helena, an attorney who lost her husband, Hank, after a long struggle with heart problems, thought she was doing fine. Her late husband's best friends, Chris and Judy, checked in regularly to see how she was doing. When she repeatedly told them she was fine, they knew she was coping in the only way she knew how.

A month following the death, her friends asked her to dinner and wanted her to choose the night.

"I'm flexible," she said. "My calendar is empty, so you pick a night and I'll be there."

They decided to get together on Monday, five days from when they placed the call. But on Monday morning, Chris called to change the date. "We're having a busy week," he told Helena. "Is Saturday okay instead?"

Helena was strangely quiet. Then she said, "I'm sorry. Saturday won't work. Let's just skip the whole thing. I have to go now." And she hung up the phone.

It turned out that Helena was devastated by what she considered a betrayal and she refused to answer a string of phone calls from Chris's wife, Judy. Judy kept leaving messages that said, "What's up? Did Chris offend you in any way? Why won't you return my calls?"

Judy even dropped by Helena's house on Friday after work to make sure Helena was okay, but no one answered the door. When she spotted a neighbor watering her garden, Judy asked her if she'd seen Helena recently.

"I saw her this morning," the neighbor said. "She was on her way to work and we waved at each other."

"I'm so worried about her," Judy confided. "She stopped returning my phone calls after we rescheduled a dinner. Does she seem okay to you?"

Later that evening, the neighbor stopped by to see Helena, who greeted her with a smile. "Your friend Judy was here today. She was concerned about you."

Helena frowned. "She used to be my friend," she said.

When Judy called again that night, Helena picked up the phone. "Please tell me what's going on," said Judy.

"I can't believe you would cancel on me at a time like this," said Helena. "That's not how friends treat each other. I never want to see you again."

"Well," said Judy, "before you throw away our friendship of twenty-three years, you need to know that we never meant to hurt you. You had reassured us that you were completely flexible. When we saw our week getting crazy and we were both exhausted, you gave us permission to do it on any night, so we chose one when we'd have more energy. If we had known you would react like this, we never would have changed it. Please, come out to dinner with us. We miss you and we love you."

Helena burst into tears. "I'm so sorry," she said. "I haven't been myself lately. I guess I had no idea how raw I felt. But I was just putting all my emotional pain and grief into other situations."

In order to give your emotions a rest, you have to accept things as they are. You have been through a lot. Your emotions are playing out in a new terrain, with emotional lows and occasional highs that you are not prepared or equipped to handle.

The loss is not over and the pain is not gone. You had bad days before any of this happened, so don't be hard on yourself for having them now. Figure out what rests your emotions and do it without judgment: things like getting lost in movies, TV, music, a change of scenery, a trip away, being outdoors, or just having nothing to do. Find what brings you some solace and lean toward it. Even when we feel we are giving our emotions a rest, it may feel forced and awkward. But you have been in such a heightened state that anything less will feel empty. Your life has been out of balance and will be for some time. It will take time to find a new balance.

People can spend time with old friends or just spend more time with current ones. Support groups may bring new people into your world. All these things will help. Be careful not to take on new relationships with lots of emotions. You may not be ready, and they can often complicate things. Your emotions, just like your body, need to repair. If you can postpone complex or important decisions, do so. If you can't, ask for help. Invite trustworthy friends and family members to give you guidance.

A year down the road, you may still find things so emotionally draining that you need to change.

Jerry appreciated keeping his outer world the same after his internal world had been so changed by the loss of his wife. He had no emotional energy to deal with any other kind of change. His job was the same, his home was the same.

In his second year of grieving, everyone at work noticed that he looked more at peace. His boss commented that he looked happier and wondered what was going on.

Jerry said, "Ever since I moved to a new house, I feel better. I could never have done it that first year—I needed the familiarity—but in the second year, every room was an emotional trap for my loss. My house went from being comforting to being a constant emotional reminder of all I had lost. The kitchen became 'the place where Sara didn't cook anymore.' The bedroom became 'the place Sara didn't sleep anymore.' But now that everything is new, Sara lives in my heart and not in the house. At first I wondered if I was not honoring her memory. Then I realized that she was not an emotional drain in life and she wouldn't want to be one in death."

REGRETS

When a loved one dies, we are often left with many regrets about all those things we wish we had said, all those things we wish we had done. We may regret what we didn't do or didn't say. We keep going back over things we wish we'd said and things we wish we hadn't. We are all human. There are very few people who can say they don't have even a small regret. Regrets are part of loss, and you are not alone in the experience of regret.

Life is usually shorter than we hoped, and we are often unprepared for loss. So it is only natural that things will feel unfinished. We often don't have the time to completely do everything we had hoped to. Very few people feel like they got to do it all, much less do it well. We will always have a dream unfulfilled, a wish not yet granted. Chances are that no matter how much you did for your loved one, how you cared for them and loved them, there will always be something else you could have done. The "more" that we long for and crave is always there and always changing. If you do it, whatever it may be for you, something else will take its place.

Holly's only regret when she was ill was that she would not live to see her daughter grow up. She bargained with God by saying, "God, please let me have her till she is in kindergarten, then she will be okay and I will want nothing more."

Holly was granted the gift of more time. At her daughter's kindergarten graduation, she looked at her daughter and said, "Please, God, just till she is ten years old. She needs a mommy a little longer."

Holly died when her daughter was eleven, even though she

had subsequently asked God to wait till her daughter was a teenager. Her loved ones will always regret that Holly didn't get "more."

There will always be regrets. You could have watched that TV show they loved. You could have said "I love you" one more time. You could have visited an extra time.

We all know intellectually that we don't have forever. We also know we can't do it all. But intellect does not inform matters of the heart. Regrets are of the heart, the yearning for more and the chance to always do it better. Regrets will always belong to the past. And death has a cruel way of giving regrets more attention than they deserve.

The illusion of infinite time clouds our understanding of the preciousness of one another. That value grows in death as we realize all that was lost. At the funeral, your husband's childhood friend speaks of their years together as kids, and you think, "I always meant to ask what it was like growing up in Chicago." You loved her meat loaf, but what was the recipe? Maybe you heard a story your loved one told over and over again at countless dinners and parties, and now you realize you have questions about that story but no one is here to answer them. Instead of answers, you are left with regrets.

Alexander was tired of living in an apartment; he wanted to buy a home with his wife, Laura. Laura didn't just want a home, she fantasized and she dreamed of one as she went on and on about the way she would decorate it and how the backyard would look. She even talked about how people would feel when they came in her home: the warmth and the colors that would help people relax. In fact, she would happily have bought the house right away, even if they found something they couldn't afford.

Alexander, however, was the practical one. "Not yet," he'd say. "Not till we're making three times a year more than the house payment would be." His worst childhood memory was of his father and mother worrying about not having enough money for their bills.

Soon, Laura found out she had advanced stomach cancer and had only months to live. The next months were spent in hospitals and with doctors, and before Alexander knew it, she was gone. The dream house had never been discussed further because they had become so consumed with her illness. It was only after her death that he was hit with intense regret about not getting a house.

"What was the big deal?" he thought. "We could have managed. Even if she had died in her dream house, I could have sold it later. At least her dreams would have come true."

Alexander has regrets and information now that he didn't have then. How could he have known they didn't have forty years to realize their dream house and so much more? But in his regrets, emotions won over details and realities.

Dreams are often the regrets of tomorrow, and all that we hope for may not always be ours to have.

Then there are the small things. Josh always sang the same song over and over again. One day his wife gave him clear directions never to sing that song again without a shower door at his side and water falling on his face. But after his death, she'd have given anything to hear that stupid song and deeply regretted she had put a stop to the song in her husband's heart.

Besides how we lived, there is the question of how we died. And the regret is, did we have to die? What if we had done it differently, since the modern medical system is filled with choices— Eastern medicine vs. Western, aggressive treatment vs. more conservative. Did we see the doctor at the first sign of trouble, or did we assume it was nothing and wait?

No matter which choice you made, since the outcome now has been loss, you may regret not choosing whatever the other option was. We have seen people choose every possible way to deal with their illness and can tell you that most of the options that keep people up at night regretting would not have made a difference in the outcome. Knowing this is not an easy statement to hear, especially with so many books discussing cures, and commercials for hospitals and cancer treatments. But there is a difference between curable and incurable diseases, and it can provide an antidote for regrets. The truth is that in most cases, doing things differently may have changed the process but would not have prevented the death.

Do your best to make peace with as many regrets as possible. It would be unrealistic to have done everything in life. It would also be just as unrealistic to have been perfect and have no regrets. Forgive yourself. Isn't it true that if you could have made better choices, you would have? You did the best you could at that time of your life.

Sometimes grief can hold healing not only for the loss but for you as a person. If you have the courage to follow your feelings to their origin, they may be simple grief. But they may also go back to a deeper feeling. Regrets will be a part of grief, but if you follow the thread to its core, you may find a sense of wrongness that has been with you your whole life. This grief may provide the opportunity for an even greater healing.

In terms of regrets around our loved one who died, if there are things you wish you'd said, know that you can still say them in your heart to your loved one. It's never too late to say, "I'm sorry. Forgive me and I forgive you. I love you and I thank you."

After that, what else is there to regret?

TEARS

Tears are one of the many ways we release our sadness, one of our many wondrous built-in healing mechanisms. Unfortunately, too often we try to stop this necessary and primal release of our emotions. In grief we often have only two main thoughts about crying. The first is the overwhelming thought of sadness that hits us. The second is, "I must stop crying." After many people begin to cry they quickly move to stop this natural phenomenon.

Melinda was the youngest to join her town's prestigious accounting firm. She married John, one of the division managers, and while he was the manager at work, she was the decision maker at home. John's background was in human resources; he knew how to manage people and their problems. Melinda was a numbers person. She loved accounting. She liked the logic that two plus two always equals four.

After twenty years of marriage, John found out he had advanced heart disease, which made no sense to Melinda, because neither of them smoked, both ate well, and both exercised frequently. This was not supposed to be happening, and yet it was. Melinda took on John's health like a project. She researched treatments on the Internet and went to every lecture she could find. When John's health deteriorated even more, Melinda found him crying. She said, "John, stop it. Tears won't do us any good."

John tenderly said, "We have done all we could, and it is almost over, and—"

She interrupted him. "But it isn't over. There's always more to do. I don't want us to miss any treatment possibilities."

John put his hand on hers and said, "Then please don't miss us saying good-bye."

She sat down on the bed with him, holding back tears. John said, "Honey, it's okay to cry. Look at me. Even I'm crying."

"You don't understand," she said. "If I started, I would never stop." With that said, Melinda continued to hold back her tears.

People like Melinda avoid crying for fear that they might cry forever. But of course you will stop crying, even if you don't believe you will. The worst thing you can do is to stop short of really letting it out. Uncried tears have a way of filling the well of sadness even more deeply. If you have a half hour of crying to do, don't stop at twenty minutes. Let yourself cry it all out. It will stop on its own. If you cry till your last tear, you will feel released.

One night, ten years to the day after John died, Melinda lost her car keys. She had a car full of groceries and it was pouring rain. She knew she had them minutes earlier but they were nowhere to be found. She checked her purse repeatedly and lifted every bag of groceries and checked the floor. After a frustrating search, she sat down in the car. She watched the rain helplessly through the windows. She noticed the raindrops hit the window, grow, and roll down the windshield, and she began to cry. She cried until a friend picked her up. Then at home she cried again until nightfall. She cried the rest of the weekend. Her face melted with the thousands of tears she cried. She looked back on those ten years and said she felt like one of those large water towers you see outside of small towns: large, high, unreachable, and full of water.

Melinda still cries from time to time, but she now knows how illogical it was to think, "If I start, the tears will never end." Of course they end. It's the feelings underneath that never end, nor would you want them to.

We live in a society that views tears as a weakness and a face of stone as strength. Whether you cry or not may have more to do with how you were raised than with the nature of your loss. Some of us were raised with permission to cry and others were not. For some, crying privately may be okay and crying publicly is unacceptable. Whatever you were taught, the loss of a loved one can tip the scales and bring up the tears you never thought you could cry.

At times, you may start to cry as if for no reason at all. It may seem it just comes out of the blue, because you are not even consciously thinking about your loss. Unexpected tears remind you that the loss is always there. People often find they are reminded unexpectedly of a loved one and start crying in a situation they were not prepared to handle. For example, you're at work and an associate you haven't seen in a year says innocently enough, "What's new?" They have no idea what you've been through, but you are suddenly flooded with emotions. There is nothing to do except collect yourself as best you can at work and explain the only thing that really *is* new.

Hospice nurse Marion had a rule that whenever she cared for a patient for more than four months, she would attend their funeral if invited. One day, Marion's supervisor, Shelley, accompanied her to the funeral of a sweet, kind woman whom they'd cared for together during the last six months. But Shelley became concerned when she saw Marion sobbing her heart out at the funeral. She knew that Marion was scheduled to see a few more patients that day, and she feared her employee would not be ready.

As they walked to their cars, Marion's tears subsided and Shelley asked, "Are you okay to see patients today?"

"Of course," she said with a smile, and she drove off.

At the end of the day, Shelley met with Marion to check on

her. She told her she was concerned at how upset she'd seemed earlier and how hard she had cried over her deceased patient.

Marion took Shelley's hand and said, "The only way I've learned to survive this work over the last twenty years is to cry every tear I have for anyone I care about. I walked away from that funeral with no residue, just some fond memories. Some nurses and families hold in bits of sadness, like it's not enough for a real big cry."

Marion knew the importance of taking the pain inside and releasing it outside. Then she was done when her sadness was fully expressed. Unexpressed tears do not go away; their sadness resides in our bodies and souls. Tears can often be seen as dramatic, too emotional, or a sign of weakness. But in truth, they are an outward expression of inner pain.

Others have their own reactions to seeing someone crying. For those around the person crying, people may feel grateful the person is able to cry. Or they may feel uncomfortable, thinking, "If they cry, I might." Or "If Cindy, who never cries at anything, is crying, things must really be bad." These days, even men are learning it is okay to cry. After 9/11 we were flooded with images of men crying, even firefighters. It helped us to view crying not as a sign of weakness but rather as an expression of deep sorrow.

Norman, a pilot, lost his only brother in the Vietnam War. He felt he needed to show his inner strength in the army base and also in his inner base at the time. Years later, 9/11 struck him deeply and personally. Besides his feelings of being a part of the country to which it had happened, it brought up all his feelings for his brother. He looked at all the men crying and thought, "I would have cried if I'd known I could." He then asked himself a rhetorical question: "So what if I had cried?" And cry he did.

Our perception about crying in public is cultural. In some

places, not crying is a sign of dignity, whereas in other cultures, not crying for the deceased is considered a sign of dishonor.

A mother survived two of her three children. When the first one, a son, died, she was so overcome by grief she fell on the casket and cried out loud. Her husband gently pulled her to her feet and the funeral continued.

When her second child died, her own mother took her grieving daughter aside before the funeral and said, "Don't make a scene like you did last time. The tears will ruin your makeup. Do you have any idea how your face looked the last time with mascara running down your chin?"

She faced her mother and said, calmly, "Do you have any idea what will be ruined if I *don't* cry?"

Tears are a symbol of life, a part of who we are and what we feel. They live in us and through us. They represent us and reside in our pain. This symbol and representation of sadness can appear anytime. Since it is so tied to life itself, we are often surprised when laughter breaks spontaneously through tears.

The humanity we witness often causes us to laugh at ourselves, but never mistake laughing through tears as a reason to feel guilty. It is the life we have, mixed with the sadness we feel. It is a fail-safe mechanism we have for managing the pain.

In grief groups we often have a rule: "Everyone has to grab their own tissues." Sometimes when someone starts to cry, everyone grabs the tissue box and shoves tissues at them. While this may be an act of comfort, it often sends the message "hurry and stop crying." Also, if we go into the role of caretaker, we avoid our own emotions.

The truth is that tears are a symbol of life and can be trusted. One woman shared how she was crying on the phone to her parents after she lost her husband. When her mother heard her sobs, she said, "We should get off the phone now." Luckily, her father jumped in and said, "No. I'm staying on the line even though she's crying."

Acceptance of death is part of the work that must be done if we are to grieve fully. If crying is part of our outer culture or inner sadness and we have tears to cry, then we should use this wonderful gift of healing without hesitation.

Long periods of denial are worse than crying. Crying is much better, but you have to cry your own tears because no one can do it for you. If you see someone else crying and you cry, it is triggering some sadness you feel inside. Sometimes you'd rather cry for any situation but your own, but regardless of your preferences, you are always crying for yourself.

ANGELS

A woman in her early forties lay in her hospital bed with her husband by her side. They both looked up as the hospital chaplain entered the room. They talked for a while about her cancer and the possible treatments. Since her cancer was advanced, she had very few treatments to choose from. She looked at her husband and then over at the chaplain and said in a very matter-of-fact tone, "Last night I saw angels. I never saw angels before."

The chaplain asked, "What were they like?"

"Oh, they were so beautiful," she said, with sparkling eyes. She looked at her husband, who did not look reassured by her vision. "Don't worry," she said, "they'll be there for you when the time comes. They will comfort you."

The chaplain ran into her physician outside the room and asked how she was doing medically. Her physician discussed her limited options but said there was an experimental treatment that might give her some additional time. When the doctor asked the chaplain how his visit went, the man replied, "She saw angels."

The doctor looked down. "That's never a good sign," he told the chaplain.

"Yes," the chaplain said, "not medically. But spiritually, it's perfect."

When the woman died, those words "They will comfort you" were like a cushion for her husband's grief. He confided in a close friend, "I can't describe it and I don't want people to think I am crazy, but I can feel it. The moment she died, I knew she was all right, and I have felt watched over ever since that moment."

Some people have strong beliefs in angels, guardian angels, while others hope they exist. We speak of them in many forms in our culture: the angel of death, angels we pray to for help and comfort. Sometimes they are just a part of our God and the heavens. We ask them to be gentle as they take our loved one. We ask them to watch over us. We ask them to meet our loved ones on the other side. Many times we just ask for their help.

It is unnecessary to debate the reality of angels. They are beyond an entity that can be proved or disproved. After a loved one's death, we often ponder the idea of them for the first time in our life. They give us hope and they comfort us. They are part of a religious and spiritual belief system that many hold dear. As much as people like to think of angels as New Age, interpretations of them and references to them go back to the book of Genesis. As God describes his creations, he uses the word "I." Then at one point he says "we." Many interpret this to mean angels of God were there before creation.

Many believe you cannot die alone, that angels are always present. Young children often refer to angels as their playmates.

They have been called everything from guides to spooks, because they can be scary if you aren't expecting them. It is not important what label we give them, but it is important to understand that many cultures believe that from the moment of birth to the end of physical existence, we are in the presence of angels who are there to help us with our last breath. They will wait till the end of our physical existence and help us transition to our purely spiritual existence. They will be there for those we leave behind. And just as you cannot die alone, you cannot grieve alone.

While many think of angels as visions of cherubs from heaven, they also appear in physical form through us and in us. Those dying and those who have experienced a deep grief will talk about how a friend was "an angel" for coming over at just the right moment.

Two sisters who were not close through the years were drawn together by the loss of one of their husbands. The other sister told her grief-stricken sibling, "We would love for you to move in with us for a while."

The widow told friends years later, "I didn't stay long, but when she gave me a place in the world when I felt so lost, I realized my sister was truly an angel."

We need to know that as the physical form of our loved one leaves, something beyond them lingers and comforts us, something beyond our ability to describe or substantiate. Grieving people sometimes say, "In my darkest days, I must have been carried by angels." They may feel it was their loved one still comforting them from a world beyond their sight. Others think angels were sent by God to reassure them that they were not alone.

Your loved one still exists. On the long road you now walk alone, you have unseen companions.

In our work with the grieving, people are very grateful for

help. We, like many others, have both felt awkward at times when someone talks about something we said in an exchange about grief and says it "changed" his or her life. Our awkwardness comes from our not remembering those life-changing moments. Whenever anyone does a pure and angelic deed for others, that person is usually unaware of it.

In the classic Frank Capra movie *It's a Wonderful Life,* an angel shows a man how much his simple yet kind deeds have done for others and what a tragedy it would be if he had never been born. The subplot of the movie concerns the angel's getting his wings for helping Jimmy Stewart's character. But the real story is that the man had never been aware of how the moments of his life had truly been angelic to others. We all have angelic moments that we give to each other. They appear as simple acts of kindness, which may seem not to matter that much, but they save lives by lifting others from sadness.

While angels watch us, we are capable of being each other's angels. In deep grief we may wonder, "Where are my angels?" while we miss all the angelic people around us. We may not be seeing or feeling all the love they bring. We may not understand that they are indeed our angels when a friend or even a perfect stranger says just the right thing at the right time.

Elliot was enjoying golfing in his retirement. One day he had a heart attack on the green and died. His wife, Connie, was devastated that her beloved husband died without her in the emptiness of a golf course. "I just wish I knew he was okay when he died. I knew he loved golf, but I wonder how he would feel about the green as a place to die."

Eleven months later Connie was overwhelmed with the task of doing her taxes. She picked up the phone and called the tax person from her husband's address book. Before she could go into an explanation of her husband's death, the tax person told her, "Your husband said you are so good with money, one day you will take over the finances."

"He said that about me?" she asked.

"Yes, he said, 'One day you will get a call that my wife is going to do the taxes this year and I will be in golf heaven.' "

Not sure if her accountant was consoling her, she asked, "What do you mean by 'golf heaven'?"

The puzzled accountant replied, "I guess it means he loved to golf, you know, like going to heaven." He continued, "Let me guess, he is off golfing now?"

She broke the news to her accountant that he had died. The man quickly apologized for the conversation, but Connie told him it was fine. She felt in a strange way that this conversation was a message from her husband that he was okay with his death. Filled with a sense of well-being and self-confidence, Connie took a deep breath and did her taxes. She not only felt that this accountant she had never met was an angel in disguise, but she also felt encouraged by her late husband.

The question ultimately may be, "What does an angel look like?" The answer is different for everyone, since we all grieve differently and are comforted differently. For some, a vision of angels will let us know that we will survive. Or we hear a voice through our sadness that reassures us. It may be the loved ones who gather to comfort us. As in Connie's case the angel may even be a stranger.

If you are expecting to see the movie version of an angel with wings, you will be disappointed. But if you look closer through your grief at the moments of your life, you may see moments that you know for sure were angelic in nature.

Angels are the extraordinary coming through the ordinary. We need them more than ever in grief, and they always come to help.

DREAMS

Dreams are a natural part of sleep. They embody our hopes, our worst fears, and everything in between. After a loss, it is not unusual to dream that your loved one is still alive. After her husband died, a woman dreamed there was a knock on the door to tell her there had been a mistake at the hospital. Someone else had died; it was a terrible mistake and her husband was alive, recovering, and on his way home.

In the next moment of her dream, her husband was stepping out of the front seat of an ambulance with sirens blaring as if to herald the enormity of the mistake made. He walked toward her looking healthy and whole. She was overjoyed as she looked into his eyes while the sirens continued to blare—until the sirens became the sound of her alarm clock.

Dreams often make promises they can't keep, a trick of our psyche that brings with it a fleeting feeling of reconnection. Many people say that regardless of the outcome of the dream, they are grateful for even a few more moments with a loved one.

Dreams can provide information about what is really going on inside us. Often people will have dreams in which they are overcome by a sense of overwhelm. A man who lost his wife said that in his dream, he was at the gym, where someone kept piling more and more weights for him to lift. "Too much, too fast," he yelled out loud as he awakened.

Our dreams can demonstrate the inevitable lack of control we feel when we are grieving. One woman who lost her sister dreamed of being caught in a storm with no way out. That one was easy to interpret, but some dreams are more difficult to read.

Dreams may serve many purposes, including a distraction

from pain or a demonstration of the soul grappling with reality. Regardless of their meaning, dreams help us deal with incomprehensible feelings while we sleep, an aid to the grief process, as the unconscious mind cannot distinguish between a wish and reality. Perhaps you are aware of illogical dreams in which two completely opposite realities exist side by side. For instance, you can be very angry in a dream that your loved one has died. At the same time you can be discussing it with them as they appear fully alive in the dream, an illogical and unthinkable experience in our waking state.

After a loss, the need to feel that our loved ones still exist somehow, somewhere, can be very important. Dreams are a very private way to find some reassurance when our world of logic can offer us none. We may not realize how much we work out psychologically in our dream state. Consider the fact that all of us dream every night, but only a small percentage of us are aware of our dreams after we awaken. Dreams can become a meeting place between the world of the living and the realm of the deceased.

Before the loss, people agree that most dreams are hard to understand because their messages are not clear. There are many symbols to be interpreted, and we are left wondering about the fragmented movie we saw in our mind. After a loss, however, dreams often change. Messages are usually much more to the point and contain signs of reassurances, continued existence, and emotional support. Even when the message is not clear, the person in grief awakens from dreams of loved ones feeling grateful. Even if their visit occurred only in the dream world, it still provides a respite from the current world of pain and loss.

Our dreams show us that our loved one is not in essence the sick person to whom we tearfully said good-bye in the hospital.

Neither is he or she the body we saw at the funeral home. Our loved one is healthy and intact, the person we knew and now long for. In some cases, dream visitations bring frustration when we can't control them. Some want to dream and cannot. They suffer as they long for the experience of dreaming of a loved one. Some may not dream at all; others may dream frequently and yet there is no deceased loved one in their dreams. It can seem even emptier with a loved one absent from life and from dreams. Some people have reported that by thinking of a loved one before bed or flipping through a photo album, they can increase the chances of a loved one's appearance. Dreams can be elusive, and you can't request a dream of your loved one and be sure it will happen. And when it does happen, you can't control the content or the duration of the dream or force it to return during dreamless periods. Even so, some people report searching for dreams to return, just as others find themselves in crowds searching for a loved one.

Even if dreams of loss truthfully reflect the circumstances around loss, they rarely follow the actual events. A long struggle may produce a dream about finding your way through the darkness in the forest to get to your loved one. A violent death from a car accident may affect your dreams by showing you a loved one sitting in the car, alive and with friends, while the interior of the car is made from casket fabric.

When people dream of a loved one, they often report feeling a sense of peace afterward, a reassurance beyond words. Some have pangs of pain at first waking when they realize it was only a dream, but eventually, the dreams will begin to subside and become less frequent. While they are still happening, they often represent a form of communication, reassurance, and emotional support from seeing the one person we desire the most.

The dream vision of a loved one can also represent unfinished business, the chance to complete something that was suddenly severed.

Dreams offer us the opportunity to say good-bye and to finish business.

They also allow us to give and receive permission for a loved one, and us, to find peace.

HAUNTINGS

Joyce was walking down Market Street in San Francisco about three months after her close friend Michael had died. She was surprised when she spotted a man she thought could easily have been Michael, with the same hair and body type. Even his walk was the same.

She watched him for a few moments and then gave in to an irrepressible urge to follow him. As she walked behind him, she kept imagining running up to him as she longed for the familiar face she missed so much. But she deliberately stayed a distance behind, realizing she didn't want to catch up to him and ruin the illusion. The possibility, no matter how far-fetched, that he was alive and was walking a few feet in front of her was comforting enough. When she eventually let him go, she was uplifted by her experience and realized she had undergone a "visual haunting."

There are many types of hauntings, such as sounds you hear, people you see, words that echo, and even the physical sensation of being touched. You can be haunted by an event in the present or the past, or by something you wish would happen in the future. Whether they are comforting or disturbing, hauntings are a part of loss that needs attention.

To feel loss is to feel a sorrow beyond lifting. A haunting is often a recurrence of the trauma of that loss, such as a vision you cannot get out of your head. Most people are haunted by something or someone. You may be tormented by a scene you wish you hadn't witnessed, like a loved one with tubes sticking out of everywhere, the smell of the hospital room, or the pained expression on your loved one's face. Maybe you can't shake the way she looked when she was diagnosed. Or when she was dying. Or after she died.

Whatever it is, the loved one is gone but the visions remain. Often, though, hauntings are helpful, as they can provide motivation to do whatever it takes to get the vision out of your mind and get you back into the world. You can talk about the visions or draw pictures of them. Art therapy can help people give physical form to their visions as these move from mind to canvas. Whatever your vision may be, find a way to get it out. Try to externalize it. Talk about it. Write a letter.

Hauntings can also be emotional. Many people are relentlessly haunted by two regretful phrases: "if only . . ." and "what if . . ." What if they'd acted faster . . . ? If only they'd had more time . . . But these regrets are part of an emotional haunting we must allow to pass before we can accept the loss.

For some, the haunting is a feeling in the room, a presence that seems like a loved one hovering, a beloved soul lingering. The truth is that such feelings and sensations are beyond explanation. We simply need to acknowledge that the feelings are real, and if the presence feels unsettling, there is some unfinished business at hand. A mother in despair will suddenly report she felt a small hand on hers. A wife going for her first job interview after her husband's death will say she felt her husband give her a sweet push forward to open the door.

In many cases, a sudden voice calling a loved one's name tenderly has soothed a grieving person in the night. Maybe the voice tells you, "I still exist. I am not gone. I will love you forever." Or it may ask for forgiveness or accept it from you.

Hauntings may be signs that you will be okay, or more specifically that it is okay to live again, to find happiness again, and even to find love again. A woman once spoke about feeling haunted whenever she smelled fresh grass being cut. She had hired a neighborhood teenager to do the job when her husband died, so the task was handled, but no one could eliminate the lingering scent that invaded her world.

It is important to remember that hauntings after the death of a loved one are normal and common. They often bring important messages from the psyche that arise from our inner world of grief. They may even bring fear with them, but they usually are not dangerous. Among the myriad of feelings connected with grief, hauntings contain valuable clues, threads to be followed to their source. They represent some unfinished business in some cases and offer great comfort in others.

After four-year-old Robbie's grandfather died, his father did his best to console Robbie. Late one evening after dinner, his father heard the young boy talking in his room. When he went to see what was going on, he found Robbie standing there smiling to himself.

"What are you doing?" his father asked.

"Talking to Grandpa," Robbie answered.

His father gave him a hug and said, "I miss him too," assuming that his four-year-old was dealing with the effects of loss. "But he's in heaven now."

"Not yet," Robbie corrected his dad. "He was just here and he told me how much he misses me. Oh yeah, he told me to tell you he's okay and the cancer is gone."

Whether or not hauntings are physical realities is irrelevant to the grief process. Anything that comforts or guides you in your grief work is naturally valuable.

To spend time questioning the experience is to miss the point . . . and perhaps the gift.

ROLES

In our lives we play many roles. We are the wife, husband, child, and parent. We are also the bill payer, gardener, organizer, mess maker, student, teacher, cook, compliment giver, criticizer, and confidante. We may be the repair person, movie partner, travel companion, clothes chooser, car repairman, and on and on.

When a loved one dies, all the roles they fulfilled are left open. Some we consciously or unconsciously take on ourselves. For other roles, we consciously or unconsciously assign them to someone else, or someone may take them on. Still other roles may be left unfilled.

Michael and his wife, Melissa, owned a small graphic design firm. He was the designer and she managed the finances, ran the office, and made the appointments. When Melissa was diagnosed with pancreatic cancer, they had no idea how quickly the cancer would spread and take her life. One month after she died, a phone call came from the bank. His account was overdrawn and they had returned five checks.

Michael realized that while his wife had been ill, he had not sent out any invoices for the last three months. As a result, no one had paid him and there was no money in the account. He completely broke down in tears. "The cancer happened so fast," he recalled, "she didn't have time to teach me how to do this. She took care of everything since we started this business, and I don't know what to do."

Michael realized he had not only lost his wife of twenty-two years but he had also lost the vital role she had played in their world. He tried to do some of what she had done, but stopped in frustration, knowing it wasn't his area of expertise. He tried to hire someone to help but could never find "anyone good." And then, on some level, the idea of having anyone take over his wife's role felt uncomfortable for him and almost a betrayal.

After the bank called, however, he clearly needed some assistance if he intended on keeping his business running. Michael did not want to hire anyone—he wanted Melissa back. Nevertheless, he recognized that the tasks she had done previously had to be done by someone else. He compromised, realizing that having a bookkeeper come to the office would not work for him. Instead, he took his information to an accounting agency down the street. Now he had reassigned Melissa's much-needed role in an impersonal way that he could bear.

We often don't realize the enormity of the roles that people play in our lives. Eleanor and Cynthia, friends for thirty years, had been through everything together. Both had even lost their husbands within two years of each other.

Now Eleanor and Cynthia were in their late sixties. For the past ten years they had became each other's companions, neither of them having any interest in marrying again. Cynthia died first, leaving Eleanor more alone in the world than ever. It had always felt as if they were in this together, and after Cynthia died, Eleanor began to realize the many roles that her dear friend had played in her life.

Now she went to movies alone and often had dinner alone. When the woman at the dry cleaner's asked Eleanor where she was going on vacation this year, it hit her that not only was her companion gone, Cynthia would have had the trip planned and booked by now. Every year when the holidays came Cynthia would arrange for both of them to volunteer to wrap presents and deliver them to foster homes. Eleanor was well into the holidays when she felt her friend's loud absence. She was literally broadsided by the fact that she hadn't arranged any volunteering and didn't even know the name of the agency that Cynthia had used.

In that first year, she recognized all the roles Cynthia had played in her life—friend, movie partner, companion, travel planner, holiday organizer. Eleanor had a sad appreciation for all that she had lost. After a few years, she knew that she would not find another Cynthia, but she became more involved in a large church, which filled many of the empty spaces. With different groups in the church, she traveled once a year and she participated in many volunteer activities. In the end, no one person could fill all the roles that Cynthia had played in Eleanor's life. It took an entire church community.

Often, we take on our loved one's roles without conscious awareness. Charlotte was a studious type. She taught school and spent most of her free time reading. Her husband, Sam, had been a stand-up comedian with the unique gift of seeing the humor in any situation and making others laugh. He was the ultimate jokester, with several stories always ready to tell, making Charlotte laugh every day. When he died of heart failure, Charlotte found her world suddenly without humor.

Six months later when her daughters were having lunch with her in a Chinese restaurant, Charlotte suddenly said, "Two guys walk into a bar . . ."

The two daughters stared at each other in shock. They had never heard their mother tell a joke during the fifty-one years of her marriage. It seemed that humor was such a big part of

Charlotte's life, her husband's demise had left a large gap. All those jokes that had lit up her life were gone, replaced with a heaviness. Her life felt out of balance, but to whom could she reassign the role of humorist? Without any conscious decision on her part, she became what she missed as she took on the role herself.

When you sit with the dying and their family, the loved ones will often say that a part of them is dying too. That is true, but equally true is that a part of the one who died lives on in us. This was the case with Charlotte and Sam. To this day, she continues to tells Sam's jokes . . . and she tells them very well.

We often carry a great deal of knowledge, most of which dies with us, but not all. We are always teaching. When a writing group lost two members in two years, they often talked about how the knowledge that the two writers had was now a part of the group and made them better writers. In honor and memory of them, the two members were not replaced, and the group feels that in a certain way they are still keeping their friends alive.

Our loved ones play so many parts in our lives. Besides the obvious ones of family and friends, their individual style of playing certain roles is lost. Maybe he was the disciplinarian parent and you were the more lenient one. Maybe she was the decisive one and you evaluated things for a while. Whether tangible or vague, there are many roles that can be missed.

At a recent memorial service a minister told the congregation, "You have not lost all of the things that you loved most about your loved one. They are in you. You can carry them with you for the rest of your life."

Then he issued a challenge to the congregation. "All of you gathered here," he said, "are friends of the widow. While all the best parts of him live on in her, many of the physical roles and

61

tasks that her husband played are now left undone. Don't call and ask what you can do. Just do it. Don't go to her house this afternoon, stay for an hour, and think you've done your part. Think about how you can help her during the next year. Play a role in her grief. That will be the greatest gift you can give her."

THE STORY

When your loved one became sick, there were medical visits, case histories, and physical tests. Then they found the lump and your world immediately began to change.

Now you sit alone remembering the story of the loss. You may find yourself retelling the story to friends and family. Immediately following the loss, everyone wants to know how it happened. You tell your tale through your sadness and tears. You talk about it after the funeral. When friends come to visit, you discuss the parts of the story you continue to grapple with, like "I didn't see it coming," or "They told us she was sick, but none of us realized just how sick she was."

As time passes, however, you may see others grow weary of hearing the story, although you are not yet tired of telling it. You may not consciously notice this, but when you encounter people who haven't heard it you are grateful to have their ear.

Telling the story is part of the healing of a traumatic event, no different from the trauma of large-scale disaster. In your world it *was* a large-scale disaster, most likely the biggest you have ever experienced.

While you try to comprehend and make sense of something incomprehensible and your heart feels the pain of loss, your mind lags behind, trying to integrate something new into your psyche. It is something that moved too fast for your mind to understand. The pain is in your heart, while your mind lingers in the facts of the story, reenacting and recalling the scene of the crime against your heart. Your heart and mind are joined in one state, pain remembering pain.

Telling the story helps to dissipate the pain. Telling your story often and in detail is primal to the grieving process. You must get it out. Grief must be witnessed to be healed. Grief shared is grief abated. Support and bereavement groups are important, not only because they allow you to be with others who have experienced loss, but because they provide another forum for talking about the devastating events that befell your world. Tell your tale, because it reinforces that your loss mattered.

You are the detective, searching out things to help you understand how to put the puzzle together. In telling the story, you open up your confusion as you cover terrain that needs exploring. But there is something about taking the inner thoughts of your mind and speaking them out loud that helps put things in order. It can be the temporary scaffolding that holds up the rocked structure of your world. Telling the story helps to re-create and rebuild structure.

You will find the story changing over time; not necessarily what happened, but what part you focus on. Telling the story may also offer the opportunity for important feedback or information, as the listener may have missing pieces of the puzzle or insight you previously lacked.

Brandy's grief after her mother died was a mixture of sorrow and relief. She was relieved when they'd placed her on a respirator, ending her struggle to breathe, but Brandy faced some irreversible decisions about life support. Her mother unfortunately had not given out any advance directives concerning her critical condition with little hope of surviving. Even though the doctors found little brain activity after her mother's stroke, it was a tough reality for Brandy. But after three weeks in the ICU with no improvement, Brandy decided the artificial intervention was keeping a body alive, but that body was not her mother.

Six months later her family had grown tired of hearing her tale over and over again. They would listen to her telling the story to yet another person and they wished she would move on. One day, she and her husband were in the mall when Brandy ran into her mother's coworker from a decade prior. Her husband secretly wished she would not go into the story. Perhaps this person did not want to hear it.

Brandy basically gave her the headlines and the coworker said, "My father was in his late seventies when he got terminal kidney disease. When he was bed-bound with no quality of life, your mother said to me, 'I hope I never end up stuck on a machine.' I'm glad she died that way."

That was exactly what Brandy needed to hear. She now knew she had done what her mother would have wanted. She also knew that if she hadn't told her story over and over, she would have missed this crucial insight.

There are many instances where, if the person had gone to the doctor sooner, it might have made a difference. However, there are many more faulty assumptions that if the person had seen a doctor sooner they could have corrected his or her death, as if the death were a mistake. As our lives need validation, so do our deaths. The stories we tell give meaning to the fact that our loved one died, which is why, in American Indian cultures, stories are given the highest priority. In fact, the function of the elderly is to tell the stories of the lives and deaths of the ancestors, the stories that keep their history alive.

In days long gone, elders sat in a circle, telling the stories to the young. These stories held enormous value. Today, in our "shut up, get over it, and move on" mentality, our society misses so much, it's no wonder we are a generation that longs to tell our stories.

In working with the dying and those in grief, we often have requests from the media to talk to someone who is dying or to their family after the loss. Initially we both felt awkward about asking people to tell us what happened, but we rarely encountered a "no." People want to tell their stories; they want their lives to matter and their griefs to be heard. Many are amazed by seeing people after a tragedy or loss talk on TV about what happened.

The ways we now have in our society to share our loss become fewer as we discount grief and loss. But ultimately we learn that not telling the story and holding it back also takes an enormous amount of energy. Saying we are fine to a good friend can feel just horrible afterward. Telling our story is primal, and not telling it can be unnatural.

Our stories contain an enormous amount of pain, sometimes too much for one person to handle. In sharing our story, we dissipate the pain little by little, giving a small drop to those we meet to disperse it along the way. Our stories also contain lessons. Mildred would tell the stories of her husband's and her parents' dying at every family event. One might imagine her sharing would be a morbid event, but she wove in important parts of who her husband was. Her tales were always filled with lessons of kindness and honesty.

Sometimes a loss is so great, you need a larger platform. Sometimes people create videos, write stories and books. The mother of a female airline pilot who died in a plane crash in the Florida Everglades wrote a book she hopes to get published. It is about the crash but also about how some people used her daughter's gender as an explanation of why the plane crashed, when it came out that the cause of the crash was an explosion in the cargo hold. She wanted people to know about who her daughter was and how hard she worked to become the first female professional pilot for a major airline.

Some speak about their losses to groups. For example, a mother who lost her daughter to anorexia goes around speaking in schools about eating disorders in teenagers. The parents of a child who climbed into a trunk during a game of hide-and-seek and couldn't get out lobbied the automobile industry for glowing internal emergency latches to open the trunk from within.

When someone is telling you their story over and over, they are trying to figure something out. There has to be a missing piece or they too would be bored. Rather than rolling your eyes and saying "there she goes again," ask questions about parts that don't connect. Be the witness and even the guide. Look for what they want to know. What different angle do you see it from? Ask what the doctor thought or what her husband would say now. What if the shoe had been on the other foot? There is a great invitation for dual exploration that we often miss in the midst of grief.

FAULT

It feels as if it were somehow your fault. You were there. You saw it all happening. In your perfect hindsight so many things stand out that could have been done differently. But all events require many converging factors in order for them to happen. For example, the tumor could have been found sooner, but we don't spend our lives looking for illnesses and we don't have a medical system based on preventive medicine. It is the same when an accident occurs. There is usually more than one factor involved.

Yet you are the one left standing in the wake of your sorrow, seeing the past as something you did wrong. Yes, your loved one could have gone to the doctor sooner. He could have spent his life going every day, but that wouldn't have been living. And if he had gone more often, the illness still might not have been diagnosed in time. He could have eaten better, exercised more. You could have encouraged him, helped, even forced him.

Maybe you think *he* should have seen it coming. Maybe it's not your fault as much as it was his. The sad reality is that, despite our best or worst efforts, we all will die someday, usually sooner than we would like. Plenty of people get annual checkups and screenings of everything, only to find that something bad still happens. However healthy you think you are, remember that vegetarians die too. Jim Fixx, one of the greatest professional runners of all time, died of a heart attack. We do things hopefully because they add life to our living, but not with the illusion they will help us escape death when our time comes.

We know all this intellectually, but still we ask ourselves, "How could something have gone *this* wrong?" It had to be someone's fault, we think, and blame is something we must examine in order to find peace.

When a mother's fourteen-year-old daughter went missing, she contacted all the authorities, filed all the reports, and put her daughter's information on every conceivable Web site that deals with missing teenagers. She also called the local TV stations, got stories in the newspaper, and read lists of things that one should do to find clues. She drove to all her daughter's usual hangouts, stopping everywhere and showing everyone the missing person flyers. For three weeks, her life was a one-woman detective-search-and-rescue party, staying up day and night, looking everywhere possible. Then the call came that her daughter's body had been found two cities away in the trunk of an abandoned stolen car. The mother's immediate response was, "Oh, my God, why didn't I think of abandoned stolen cars?"

Bad things happen, illness happens, accidents happen, crimes happen, and we want to prevent them. But the truth is that life is risky and dangerous, and we are the only species on earth who knows that as much as we fear it, death will come to each of us one day.

Part of our terror comes from being bombarded with fear messages from the media. And then, when our relatively safe lives are fraught with tragedy, we look for someone to blame.

Your sorrow is the inevitable result of circumstances beyond your control, and that is always hard to live with. But in time you will get used to it and hopefully begin to see that with additional effort, the results might still have been the same. The loss would still be there even though you did the best you could, and blame is futile because it does not accurately reflect the truth about what happened. In time you will find peace and you will remember your successful role as companion, caregiver, friend, and family member. Death is inevitable, and in most cases, no one is to blame.

Lucy met her friend Stan in a coffee shop. As he was leaving he said, "If you bump into Joann tell her I'll be at the bowling alley." Later that same evening Lucy gave the message to Joann, who took off to join Stan at the bowling alley. A few hours later, Lucy's phone rang. Joann had been hit by a car just outside the bowling alley, and she died instantly. In the midst of the terrible shock, Lucy blamed herself. "If only I hadn't given her the message, she would be alive right now. It's all my fault."

Lucy took her escalating guilt to a grief counselor. He said, "When Christopher Columbus discovered America, it was the result of converging factors. There was exploration in the air and they were searching for other new routes, so if it wasn't Christopher Columbus it would have been someone else. It was just his time. It's the same with death, although it is harder to accept. But if you had not given her the message, someone else would have. Or maybe Joann would have gone looking for Stan herself."

Illness works in exactly the same way. Jeff began having slight headaches when he started managing a second area at work. He figured the headache was due to the sudden and additional stress and asked his wife, Dorothy, to pick up some Tylenol. He took them, but his headache remained. He tried to arrange relaxing evenings at home with his wife to counteract the work stress, but his headaches only got worse. He considered seeing the doctor, but when he switched to Motrin and his head felt better, he and Dorothy both figured they had worked it out.

Two weeks later, the pain came back with such a vengeance, Dorothy drove Jeff to the emergency room. Jeff feared he would be diagnosed with his mother's illness, migraine headaches, but instead he was diagnosed with an inoperable brain tumor. He lived only a few months more, and after his death, Dorothy became obsessed with wishing she had gotten him straight to the doctor. Things might have been different, she thought. Maybe if they had caught it sooner it would have been operable.

Her friends were concerned about her self-blame, and someone suggested that she make an appointment with her husband's doctor to discuss his case. She did so, and the doctor was happy to see her. When she spoke about her concerns and guilt, he told her gently, "Dorothy, I understand why you feel this was your fault, but it was a fast-growing tumor, very large by the time your husband started having the headaches. If you had come on the first day, the outcome would have been the same. I am so sorry, but you must not blame yourself or him."

Many cases are not as cut-and-dried as the one above. We are often left with vague factors, with our "what if?" mind alive and well. But how do we make the right choices? In the case of cancer, people are often faced with multiple choices for treatment options, an arena that is a perfect breeding ground for blame. No matter what you choose, no matter how much consideration you give each one, and no matter what the experts say, you still wonder, "What if we had tried one of the other options?"

We have to understand that more often than not, the most tragic of events happens and it's no one's fault. None of us knows why one person dies and another survives; such questions lead to a condition of self-blame mixed with guilt, often called survivor's guilt. But this kind of guilt has no logical basis.

This survivor's guilt concept first got widespread attention after World War II, as some concentration camp survivors wondered, "Why them and not me?" The phenomenon of survivor's guilt occurs whenever someone witnesses or survives a catastrophic experience, such as the Oklahoma City bombing, the 9/11 plane crashes, car accidents, and even widespread diseases such as AIDS. It can also strike when a loved one dies from natural causes. Although it is easy to understand why people who have lived through painful or horrific events would wonder why they had been spared, it is ultimately a question without an answer.

We have no control over certain situations, and believing that we do is a form of arrogance. It is not for us to ask why someone dies or why someone lives. Those decisions are left to God and the Universe. And yet, though there is no answer to this question, there is a reason for what has happened: the survivors have been spared in order to live.

The real question is this: If you have been spared in order to live, are you living? Can you be fully living if you don't grieve your loss?

Blame and guilt can be used, like everything else, to distract ourselves from the pain of loss. It is much easier to get involved in the whys and what ifs than it is to sit with the fact that our beloved is gone forever. Of course, you will go through self-examination, but as you do so, you will find that even the exploration cannot change what has happened. Unless it was a violent crime or gross neglect, no one is to blame.

We are responsible for our health, but we are not the ones to blame for our illnesses.

RESENTMENT

The phone rang late one evening at the Belson household. Kate answered. She heard the caller's words without any sign of emotion and then asked the caller to hold on. She yelled to her husband, "Your father is dying, what should I tell them?"

Bill replied, "Tell them to let us know when the funeral is."

On the surface the words sounded harsh. Yet Kate, Bill's wife, knew they were appropriate for the situation. Bill's father had left his family for another woman when Bill was six years old. His father and his new wife moved across the country to "start over and have a more relaxed life with so much less responsibility." Bill and his brother and sister were left to grow up without a father. Bill's father made no pretense of caring, no Christmas presents, no happy birthday wishes. Bill watched his mother work as a receptionist and do her best to make ends meet. He grew up resenting his father more than his mother did.

After the call Kate had only one question for Bill. She said, "I understand you not wanting to be at his deathbed, but why go to the funeral?" Bill, unsure of himself, said, "I guess to just say good-bye and good riddance."

71

People are often conflicted about the loss of loved ones, especially parents about whom they had mixed emotions. The major block to their dealing with and moving through the loss is that they can't understand feeling that way about someone they really didn't like, as in Bill's case. "My mother was so mean to me. She was literally a tyrant. Why do I care that she died?" one woman asked.

In a film version of Mary Shelley's famous novel, *Frankenstein,* Dr. Frankenstein gives life to the monster without any regard for the creature's happiness or what his life would be like, dooming him to misery and torment. At the end of the story, when Dr. Frankenstein is finally killed, the creature is found crying. When asked why he is crying for the man who brought him such great suffering, the creature replies, very simply, "He was my father."

We mourn for those who cared for us the way they should have. We also mourn for those who did not give us the love we deserved. We've seen this phenomenon over and over: the severely beaten child in the hospital longs for his mother but cannot see her, because she is in jail for having beaten him. You can grieve fully for people who were terrible to you. And if you need to grieve for them, you should do so. We must take time to mourn and experience our losses, and acknowledge the reality that those losses cannot be negated even if we think the person did not deserve our love.

Resentment doesn't always die with death. It can be a common part of unfinished business we are left with. Resentment is old anger that we never dealt with or had the chance to deal with. It can arise from situations as deliberate or as under the surface as Tony's.

Tony's wife, Carol, would always get mad at her kids when they didn't listen well to their father. She would tell Tony, "They have to listen to you. What if I wasn't here someday? They need to be listening to you."

A year later when Carol died in a car accident, Tony would think back on her words and struggle with resentment. He knew the accident was out of her control but often wondered if she had a premonition that she didn't share with him. And he was resentful that her words came true, that he was left with two kids and no wife. In his bereavement group he would say, "I love her, I miss her, and I resent her for dying."

Intellectually we know that people don't want to die on us, but that message does not always translate into our emotional response to the loss.

OTHER LOSSES

You cannot grieve only one loss. You may have lost your beloved, but the grief brings into your awareness all the losses that have occurred in your life, past and present. The past losses are the deaths that came before. The present losses are all the changes you have to accommodate in your life to fill the void left behind by your most current loss.

We cannot help but remember losing a parent when we were young or a high school friend killed in a car accident or any other early loss. We may feel all the grief we did not attend to before but still needs attention. What is left ungrieved remains stored in our body, heart, and soul. It can come out each time we experience loss anew.

Jillian was twenty-two when her husband, Todd, was deployed to Vietnam. They were madly in love, and after only one year of marriage he was overseas and she was a military wife, spending her time with many other wives whose husbands were away. They were all young, happy to be married, and excited about the military with all its travel and new experiences. What she hadn't counted on was her husband's being killed in action. Suddenly she was back in her hometown as if her husband and the whole military experience had been a dream.

She quickly got a job and then got a promotion to another town. She met a coworker, Jim, and married again. They were together for the next thirty-five years, and their life was full of kids, grandkids, and lots of friends. Then when Jim was killed in a car accident, Jillian was shocked and overwhelmed with grief, but not just for Jim. She was grieving his death at the age of sixty-three when she was hit with the memory of Todd, who had died when she was twenty-three. It was the first time she had tapped deeply into her storehouse of grief for the death of her first husband, which sat just beneath her sorrow for Jim. What she had considered a closed chapter was anything but.

This does not mean she loved one more than the other. It means she had two important losses to grieve, one current and one still unattended to from the past. She confided to a counselor that she felt distracted by her grief for Todd when she wanted so much to grieve Jim's death. The counselor understood and suggested she fully mourn the loss of her more current husband and stay focused on the funeral preparations. She agreed that when feelings for Todd arose, she would say to herself, "Todd, I will honor you too and I have not forgotten you. But first I must attend to mourning grief over Jim."

When the funeral was over, Jillian decided to gather all her old photographs and spend a weekend in Biloxi, Mississippi, where Todd had been stationed. She visited their old house, looked through photo albums, and cried all the tears that had been stored up in her body for forty years.

When she came back home, she felt she had honored both of their losses and now she could grieve both of them, as she had increased her capacity to feel love. She felt a great deal lighter after finally crying all the sadness she had put off for young Todd. And she felt fully present to deal with the loss of Jim and to be there for her family in their grief.

Another reason we go back to old losses is that we can visit them more easily now that we are older, deeper human beings. We have a larger palette from which to view the loss. Unlike Jillian, you may have fully grieved your losses at the time, but there is more to grieve as you continue to grow. Thankfully, we develop new tools to work with the grief.

Bill and Rodney were close brothers, less than two years apart. When Bill was twenty-one, Rodney complained of pain in his stomach. Rodney went to the doctor and got some medicine for a presumed ulcer. But that night, Rodney's appendix ruptured and he died.

Bill was lost without Rodney, and the next few years were dark and sad. He lived his life and functioned fairly well, but he always kept Rodney in his heart. When he married ten years later and began a family, Bill began to live his own life more fully and in deeper appreciation, but he felt new pain for Rodney. Now he was grieving what his brother had missed by dying young: no marriage and no kids. During this time when his friends were all hitting their forties and having midlife crises, Bill looked like he was having one too, but really, he was simply revisiting the loss of Rodney.

With every passing decade, as his kids grew into teenagers, Bill was struck with just how young his brother had been when he died. He told his wife, "I continue to understand loss better and better. I cry more deeply when I think about all that Rodney has missed. I used to tell people how I keep revisiting Rodney's death, but they didn't understand. They wanted to know why I hadn't gotten over him yet. How can I explain to them that grief is not finite? There is nothing static about loss; it keeps changing, just like we do."

The truth about loss is that the resurgence of old pain and grief has an important purpose. As the pain emerges, we find new ways of healing ourselves that may not have existed before. Return visits to old hurts are an exercise in completion, as we return to wholeness and reintegration.

Another loss is the old "you," the person you were before this loss occurred, the person you will never be again. Up till now, you didn't know this kind of sadness. You couldn't even have imagined anything could feel this bad. Now that you are inconsolable, it feels like the new "you" is forever changed, crushed, broken, and irreparable. These temporary feelings will pass, but you will never be restored to that old person.

What is left is a new you, a different you, one who will never be the same again or see the world as you once did. A terrible loss of innocence has occurred, only to be replaced with vulnerability, sadness, and a new reality where something like this can happen to you and has happened.

There are many other losses you will feel. Perhaps you were married and all your friends were married couples. Now you are a third wheel. They may try to include you and you may try to fit in, but for the most part, many people say they end up losing this set of friends. There can be only so many dinners with couples trying to bring you comfort. Whether it is an active withdrawal on their part or yours, it becomes another loss to deal with.

Another loss is the world in which your loved one lived and included you. Perhaps you were in the corporate world and your wife taught theater. On your own, you never would have gone to play openings or met actors, directors, and writers. But that was your wife's world and you had a place in it. Once she is gone, however, you have a few token dinners with colleagues and grieve together, you may still get invited to some plays, but it is not the same. You don't fit into that world anymore without your wife.

You also lose the activities you may have done together. The ritual of going to your favorite restaurant for Sunday night dinner is no more. Going on your own or with a friend doesn't feel right. Maybe you and your spouse golfed together or bowled together. Whatever activity you loved is now gone or has become a solo activity, and it will never feel the same.

For some there are financial concerns, as finding new ways to survive and bring in new income is a loss all its own. In some cases, people are forced to sell their houses, another huge loss that feels like going from insult to injury, loss upon loss.

Besides all the external losses, there are the ones that resonate within you—the loss of your beloved as a companion, a sounding board, and a life partner. She was the one to whom you told everything. She was a witness to your life. You didn't need to preface anything or give the background. You had continuity with someone you loved, someone who knew your past and discussed your friends and your work, and someone who helped you make decisions.

It is a tremendous and heartrending adjustment you must make to a new world full of losses. No one can stand where you are and survey all that you have lost. That is for you and you alone to know.

Perhaps you can take comfort in knowing that with time, you will find new ways, new things, and even new people to be with. You will discover a world of things outside yourself and inside yourself that you never knew existed.

But for now, your task is to grieve and feel this loss and all your other losses.

LIFE BELIEFS

Grief is also the shattering of many conscious and unconscious beliefs about what our lives are supposed to look like.

Many of us share certain common beliefs: that after we're born, we'll have a good childhood—or if it's a challenging one, we'll make it through and grow stronger from it. Then we will meet our special someone, get married, and find a career. We understand that we may not get the greatest job in the world, and our marriage won't be perfect, but we will love our kids and for the most part, we expect to be satisfied. Finally, when we are old and gray, we will invite the family over to look at old photo albums, tell each one how much we love them, and then, that very night, die peacefully in our sleep.

Those are our beliefs, our hopes, our fantasies, the way life should unfold. But what happens when someone gets cancer at forty? What happens when a loved one is killed in a car accident? Or a child dies? That is not the way things were supposed to happen. Life was never supposed to be perfect but was always supposed to be *long*. Disease, earthquakes, accidents, and planes flying into buildings are not supposed to happen. When these things do happen, we not only must grieve the loss, we also must grieve the loss of the belief that it shouldn't have happened at all.

How do these beliefs start? When a four-year-old child asks, "Daddy, how come people die?" the most comfortable answer is, "Because their body gets old and worn out."

That is an appropriate answer for a four-year-old, and there are few alternatives. We can say, "Son, this is a random, chaotic world, and I might have cancer right now as we speak. In fact, you might too. This could be my last day and for that matter, it could be yours."

No one expects us to say these things to a child, but as children grow, we need to update their views on life and death. If we don't, we perpetuate the beliefs and assumptions that nothing ever goes wrong. If that is the belief a child takes with her into adulthood, she will have little sense of reality and a hard time coping with life. Much like polishing a rock in a tumbler, it is the tumbling of life that makes the diamond.

When a loss hits us, we have not only the particular loss to mourn but also the shattered beliefs and assumptions of what life should be.

These life beliefs must be mourned separately. Sometimes we must grieve for them first. We can't grieve the loss if we are in the midst of "It's not supposed to happen this way." We have all seen that shock and numbness on people's faces. We intellectually know that bad things happen—but to other people, not us, and certainly not in the world we assumed we were living in.

When there is an exception to our belief system, we want to assign a reason that makes us feel safer. For instance, when someone reads about a plane crash, he might say, "Well, there are just too many planes in the sky. If we weren't flying all over the place, people wouldn't die in large numbers."

The reality is people have always died in large numbers in natural disasters such as avalanches, earthquakes, and tornadoes. But in our current belief system, we don't find anything natural about them.

Even the belief that a child is not supposed to get sick and die, that a child's death is unnatural, is not a reality. If you look back a hundred years, infant mortality rates were very high and were considered a part of life. If you had seven children, you knew that only a few would survive. That was reality.

Today we believe that modern medicine can cure anything that ails us, and we relax into that belief. Aaron was the youngest and strongest of his five brothers. By the time they reached their thirties, Aaron was very athletic, a healthy eater, and he nagged his brothers to be the same. They just weren't interested in exercise and didn't care about their physical health, but they admired Aaron's dedication.

You can only imagine the shock and devastation when Aaron, at age thirty-one, was diagnosed with advanced colon cancer. After his death, they could not explain how this had happened to Aaron, the only brother of the six who took good care of himself.

In essence, they were struggling with their crushed belief system that if they did the right things, they would have a good result. It is easy to understand this assumption until we remember that athletes die too—and they have heart attacks. It leaves us to wonder, why bother trying to be healthy? The answer is that healthy living can prevent some conditions from developing or being exacerbated. But the belief that healthy living will stop us from dying is a hard belief system to hold together when we are deep in grief.

In the grieving process, we also need to take time to mourn the life we were supposed to have. We need to honor our loss by reminding ourselves that "It didn't happen to someone else, it happened to me." Take the time to live with the question of "Why me?" For some the answer is "Why not me? Why should I be excluded from life's losses?"

Your belief system needs to heal and regroup as much as your soul does. You must start to rebuild a new belief system from the foundation up, one that has room for the realities of life and still offers safety and hope for a different life: a belief system that will ultimately have a beauty of its own to be discovered with life and loss.

Think of a lifeless forest in which a small plant pushes its head upward, out of the ruin. In our grief process, we are moving into life from death, without denying the devastation that came before.

ISOLATION

You are alone. There is a wall now where none existed before, standing between you and the rest of the world.

But your isolation is not related to your surroundings or the people in your world. You can be in a large group of friends and relatives and feel as disconnected as if you were lost in the desert. There is no port in this storm, and the one person who could bring you connection is the one person who is gone forever. And so, you feel you will be forever lost.

Friends are concerned that you have shut down and seem disconnected from the outside. In fact, this kind of isolation over an extended period of time may be cause for alarm, and indeed you may need help. But feeling isolated after loss is normal, expected, and healthy. Even when friends urge you to talk about it (they are certainly being caring), you wonder what there is to say. Sometimes people's desire to deliver you from your isolation may have more to do with their own fear and discomfort than with a concern for yours.

How can your friends not understand that your loss has shut you down and that isolation comes with a profound silence all its own? You have entered an abnormal, lonely, and unwelcome new world where you are nothing but an island of sadness. And so far, there is no way out, no matter what anybody else wants for you.

Lily was terribly isolated after her husband and two children were killed by a teenager in a car, rushing to a class. She sank heavily into isolation, and after months of no apparent change, a group of well-meaning friends did an intervention. They appeared at her house one Tuesday evening, and she opened the door without surprise or emotion. They explained their concern and she said, "I feel a kind of isolation that you'll never be able to understand. What you see is a mere fraction of what's happening inside, but at least my inner and outer worlds are reflecting each other. You wouldn't want me to throw my worlds off balance, would you?"

"But maybe going out into the world and doing things would help," her closest friend suggested. "Wouldn't you like to try?"

Lily stared off into space. "That might work for you, but I need to be where I am right now. I love you for caring and I don't expect anyone to understand. All I can say is that I know there will come a time to live again, but this is not the time."

For Lily, isolation was an important tool for grieving, as it brought harmony to her inner and outer realities. She instinctually knew this, and she also knew that getting back out there was premature for her. And she knew the time would come.

The death of a loved one often leaves you isolated symbolically as well as physically. You were with someone and now you are not. You thought for two, you planned your meals around someone else, maybe you were siblings together, lovers together, or best friends in a million different adventures. How can you not feel isolated?

Isolation is a very important stop on the path of grief, but usually, it should only be a step along the way. When you stay too long and get stuck, healing can get further and further away. Isolating too much and for too long can result in your world becoming tighter and closer, until you can literally become paralyzed.

A lack of an expressive outlet is one of the toughest parts of isolation. With anger, you can get mad at someone and yell. With sadness, you can cry. But isolation feels like being in a room with no doors or windows—a place with no way out. And the longer you get stuck there, the harder it becomes to share the pain and sorrow that create the portals for your movement into the next phase of grief. In isolation, hope disappears, despair rules, and you can no longer glimpse a life beyond the invisible walls that imprison you.

Some people find it helpful to work gently at propelling themselves back into the world. In one case, a woman reported that after four miserable forced lunches with friends, she suddenly enjoyed the fifth one as she found herself laughing at a joke, even after all she'd been through. For people who cannot push themselves, however, bereavement groups are a good antidote for isolation. They allow you to maintain a sense of privacy and aloneness while at the same time, they offer the opportunity for connection in a safe and controlled way.

In time, you will find a bridge back to the outside world. For many, a good way is to talk to others who have experienced loss, another recommendation for bereavement groups. When you feel isolated and you find yourself sitting next to someone who feels the same way, you start to feel a little less so. Perhaps the two of you actually replace some of the isolation with a sense of bonding.

Billy felt completely isolated while his mother was dying. Everyone around him was experiencing their own grief, assuming that at ten years old, Billy had no capacity for grief as yet. Of course, that wasn't true. If you are old enough to love, you are old enough to grieve. Grief just looks different in children, and during his mother's hospital stay, although it concerned the social worker, Billy found solace sitting alone on the stairwell.

The problem was that while his mother lay on the verge of death, he was not eligible for a bereavement group. One day, a woman whose husband was also in the intensive care unit passed the boy on the stairwell. She said hello and kept on walking, not wanting to intrude on his solitude. But later that day, she came and sat down next to him, in overwhelm from her own grief. "Can I be alone with you here?" she asked.

Billy nodded. For the next few days, they would spend time together on the stairwell, just the two of them, talking about loved ones occasionally but spending much of the time in silence. Both families thought that Billy and his new friend were isolating themselves. They were, but it was the healthiest thing they could do, as their isolation became their point of connection. In fact, the bond they forged that was born out of loneliness and tragedy became a friendship that lasted for the next twenty years.

This wise woman understood that grief in children feels different than it does in adults. Kids don't have the words or permission to voice their grief, while adults have trouble expressing the emotions. But whatever one does to survive and manage the grief, being alone often feels safer than being vulnerable with people who may not understand.

As in the case of Billy, isolation is not always an obstacle. Rather, it can be a necessary way station.

If it's time for you to move beyond the isolation, here are some ways to begin: Call a friend and ask for suggestions or companionship. Introduce an activity into your isolation like painting, gardening, or walking. Nature has a way of healing the soul.

Besides bereavement groups, which we mentioned above, there is private counseling for those who are not drawn to interacting with groups of others as yet. If you are ready to venture out a bit, try sitting at the back of a class or a group activity and see how it feels. At first, of course, it may feel forced until something sparks your interest.

Isolation is part of your grief and may serve as an important transition back into life. Ultimately, isolation is a darkness to experience, but not a place in which to live.

SECRETS

We all have secrets, some big and others quite insignificant. Regardless of the size, they are ours and for whatever reason we have chosen not to share these bits of information.

After a loved one has died it is not unusual to uncover a secret or two here or there. The hardest part is that the secret represents something we perceive as them withholding from us personally. It may be very painful to find out a loved one had a gambling habit or strayed from a marriage. Secrets can leave behind more than just a bit of information. They often leave many questions in their wake. Sometimes the secret our mate or sibling hid from us may be about their past before they met us or before we were born. The truth about life is that we don't usually share all of what we have done or where we have been.

A tremendous shock arises when a secret is discovered. Sometimes you must take time to deal with the shock separately from the grief. In many ways there are two forms of grief to deal with: the loss of the person you loved and your reaction to the secret. This reaction is often a component of grief. The sadness, anger, resentment, betrayal, or mystery it leaves in its wake must be felt on its own.

Not all secrets are negative in nature. Loved ones are shocked to find that someone about whom they thought they knew everything had a secret hobby or passion. People will often encounter a part of their loved one that was positive and be equally puzzled that they didn't share that part of themselves. It is an illusion that we know everything about each other or that we even should.

If you try to keep a secret, such as the circumstances around a death, perhaps suicide, it may cause a barrier between you and receiving support in your loss. When a loss is acknowledged by another, instead of receiving the care, you hear the secret or lie you created. That secret may make it difficult to find healing in the situation.

Just as people have secrets in their lives, they also have them in their deaths and grieving. For some, to grieve is to be weak. They have the misperception that to grieve is not to be able to handle a sorrowful situation. But when people hide their grief, it becomes a secret in itself. How many times has someone appeared to show no emotions, acted like nothing was wrong, and kept their grief a secret? We say, "How can they be doing so well?"

There are certain cases, however, when for whatever reason, we must keep grief a secret. A funeral director spoke about how every once in a while he would have what he called "after hours." He was referring to the times he got a call from the ex-wife, the mistress, the illegitimate son, the black sheep of the family, the one who would not be welcomed to grieve at the funeral.

A woman named Joyce shared how she married young and her marriage ended in a mutually agreed upon divorce. Both she and her ex-husband went on to remarry and have other families, but Joyce said, "I never stopped loving him. He was my first love, my first marriage. I would never dare tell him, for I wouldn't want to harm my family or his, but he knew anyway.

"When he died I wanted to cry for him but I felt that as the ex-wife, I needed to keep a low profile for his family. I wanted to honor my deep, deep sadness without any disrespect, so I called up the funeral director and told him my problem. He accommodated me and let me show up at the funeral home after hours."

In many situations, for many reasons, we sometimes feel that people should not show their grief. Whether the hiding is valid or necessary isn't really the issue. The issue is that hiding grief and keeping the secret makes grief more complicated to deal with.

People sometimes decide to keep secret the cause of the death of a loved one. They may think the real reason was unacceptable, as when a son dies of AIDS and the family says he had cancer. When and why people do this is often a mystery to others around them. There may be a clear prejudice or there may not. For example, when an elderly woman died of pancreatic cancer, her son wanted everyone to think it was pneumonia. For some reason he thought pneumonia was acceptable and cancer was not. We are also seeing this with Alzheimers. People may find some behavior embarrassing, but that doesn't mean we should be ashamed that our loved one has the disease.

Josh was in his midfifties when he had financial problems that were so severe, he took his own life. His wife told everyone it was a heart attack, since the story of a man "who had a full life and suddenly died" was much better than that of a man who had taken his own life. But what price did this widow pay for her secret? Her grief became so much harder to handle when well-meaning friends would say to her, "At least it was sudden and he had a good death."

Her perception that he did not have a good death became a secret that only added to her pain. Loss is hard enough without burdening yourself with a secret. If you can't be completely honest with the general public, find at least one or two people who can witness your grief honestly and openly.

In most cases, a secret lives long after a death occurs. Marshall was a good husband. He and his wife, Cynthia, a housewife, mother, and grandmother, had a long and satisfying marriage for forty years. After Cynthia died, the family was going through some old trunks and found many awards she received during her college years for journalism and speech. She'd even won a statewide speech contest, and Marshall was shocked that his wife had so much talent and had never said a word.

He was left wondering what it meant that she had a gift but didn't choose to pursue it. Did he not provide an atmosphere in their marriage for her to express such talent? He would never know the answer, but he hoped she was happy with him. He just hoped she was happy with who she had become and didn't long for a dream unfulfilled that could have been. He just knew he would like to have known more about her. He struggled in his grief with her secret and the question: did she not tell or did he not ask?

A secret ultimately doesn't change the person you knew. Every facet of a diamond is real, but each is a different view, so don't let all that you held dear about your loved one be negated by some other part of them. What you knew was real. What you found out was most likely real also. If it was negative, do your best to realize they were merely mortal just as you are. Forgive them if you need to, and try to accept the parts of them you didn't know. Death can invade our privacy and deprive us of the chance to explain our actions.

As hard as it may be to understand, the withholding of a secret is usually not about you. It is about your loved one's keeping a part of themself just for the sake of their own identity or maybe not feeling good about a part of their own life. Perhaps keeping the secret actually gave them pleasure. You may feel that you would have understood had you been given the chance. You may be angry that you weren't given the chance. That makes perfect sense, since death robs us of our chances at many things, including the chance to redeem ourselves if that was our intent.

Your loved one may never have intended to share all of herself with you. If you think about it, you most likely did not share all of yourself as well.

Just imagine the shoe being on the other foot. What if you had died? Are there secrets your loved one would find out about you?

Many people find compassion for their loved one when they think about the tables being turned on their secrets.

PUNISHMENT

What did you do so wrong to deserve this kind of punishment? What did your loved one ever do to deserve their illness and death? Nothing. But that does not stop us from feeling punished.

"If I had been a better person, maybe this wouldn't have happened." Or maybe you realize your imperfections but feel that "the crime doesn't fit the punishment." It doesn't. We live under the assumption that if we are just, we will not suffer. But to have life is to know death. To love is ultimately to lose what we have had the privilege of loving.

For some, the idea of punishment may come from religion and a God that punishes. Actions have consequences, but as counselors we do not believe that loss comes from punishment.

In the light of loss, all our transgressions may feel illuminated and we may feel punished, but an all-loving God would not bestow such pain on us. Death may follow life, but punishment is not God's consequence for loving and caring.

Sometimes the memory of punishment goes all the way back to our childhoods. It is not unusual to hear someone say, "I feel punished, but I can't remember what I did to deserve this kind of pain."

Robert was pleased that the tumor near his spine was removed and he was now cancer free. He talked about what a gift cancer was, which is common among people who go into remission. Others with cancer disagree, saying if cancer was a gift, they would give it back. But what Robert was really talking about was the gifts that he got from facing death. He talked about how he had felt punished for his life but now he had turned over a new leaf. He began reading books on curing ailments and articles on how negative thinking or the lack of positive thinking affects us and we create our own illnesses. He studied diets that promised to keep him cancer-free, did prayers in the morning and meditation at night, and he returned to church.

The problem was that he was not doing these things out of a sense of love for himself or his community. He was doing them out of fear as he bargained, "God, if I give you all of this, then will the cancer not come back?"

Robert was sure he had beaten it because of all his hard work, but a year later they found another lump in his abdomen. He felt completely defeated and punished. "What did I miss?" he kept asking himself as he started chemotherapy. "I thought I was cured, but what spiritual lesson is this? Why am I being punished again?"

We have many rounds with diseases in this life, and the common language we use is that we "beat" our disease and "win" the battle. But if the reality is that we are all destined to die someday, does that mean the disease wins and we lose? Some people believe that if they become spiritual enough, they will be able to cure their diseases. That, however, is bargaining, not spirituality! Spirituality is not a cure for disease. It's our reconnection with ourselves, with our soul, and with life, even in the face of death. It is the way we seek peace. Perhaps Robert's lesson was to accept things just as they were. Maybe he did absolutely nothing wrong and things were unfolding just as they were intended.

Finding inner peace, forgiving yourself and others, and being calmer will benefit your body, but spirituality in itself is not always a healing of the body. And falling ill does not mean that you are doing something wrong. True spirituality is not about blaming or finding fault. It's about reaching into the purest part of yourself, the part that is connected to love, the part that is (if you believe it to be) connected to God, the part that is beyond the body and health and disease. Spirituality is concerned with the mind and spirit, and the body.

In your childhood, you may have experienced a parental discipline style that included punishment as a result of a mistake, but this is different. You are different. Grief causes us to define our God and his attributes more closely. Is he a punishing God? Does he give out horrible pain for our human experience, including the mistakes that go with being human?

In our modern-day culture we have come to believe that an all-loving, all-caring God will offer us a world in which death is optional. When we are not in grief, we can see that is not true, but when life is at its toughest, it's easy to believe that God callously uses death as punishment. The reality is that God gives us a life cycle that includes death. We live in a world of duality. God created day with night, light with shadow, and life with death. You may be able to do a reexamination of your God by getting angry at him. Do what you need to release him as the punisher and you as the one who is punished.

That doesn't mean that your feelings of punishment aren't real. If you have lost a child, how could you not feel punished in some way? If a parent says they found meaning and did not feel punished in losing a child, it is usually years later.

Sometimes feeling punished keeps us connected to our loved ones, but there are other, better contexts in which to hold your memories.

When we look back in time, death has always been distasteful to man, and probably always will be. It may be a point on a continuum, and the soul may be eternal, but death has always been painful and associated with punishment. This can best be explained by our basic knowledge that in our own mortality, we cannot fully comprehend an ending to our own life here on earth. If this life of ours has to end, the ending is always attributed to a malicious intervention from the outside by someone or something else. Therefore death in itself is associated with a bad act or a frightening event, something that in itself calls for a retribution and punishment. So if we feel on a primal level that our own death would be a punishment, why wouldn't we feel punished with a loved one's death?

In our unconscious mind, we cannot distinguish between a feeling and a deed, just as our unconscious mind cannot distinguish between our anger at someone and a wish to kill them or be rid of them. The child who wishes his mother would leave him alone or stop bugging him will be greatly traumatized by the actual death of his mother. Even if these events are not linked closely in time, he will always take part or all of the blame for the loss. On some deep level he may feel "I did it." He may feel his anger at his mother made him responsible.

As adults, we will always make mistakes and do things we are not proud of. And on some level, if our loved one dies, we may feel like we deserve the loss: we are being punished because we weren't as loving as we could have been. There are those who channel their sense of punishment into good deeds. While it would be preferable not to feel punished in the first place, our feelings should not be denied, and some people feel that they need to work off their punishment. If they can ultimately forgive themselves, doing good in the world is much healthier than being destructive.

A chaplain noticed that people who feel punished sometimes need to confess in order to address unresolved issues. There may be a question in someone's mind as to their part in the death, and they may feel they need redemption. On a primal level, disobeying God may mean death to certain people. In fact, there is a long history in the Old Testament of a punishing God. You may need to feel the sorrow of your forgiveness or give or receive an apology in order not to get stuck. In grief we can be more connected to loss than grace. In grace we restore the relationship through forgiveness.

The saving grace of loss is that the hardships are an opportunity for growth. The first reaction to a statement like this is, "God could let me grow by taking a class, not by losing a loved one." But you are unable to see or understand this kind of growth until years into the future when you look back on your life.

The Grand Canyon was not punished by windstorms over hundreds of years. In fact, it was created by them. Your loss may feel like a punishment, but you are not the product of a God who punishes you with a loved one's death. You are a creation with the unbelievable power to weather life's toughest storms.

If someone had tried to shield the Grand Canyon from the windstorm, we would never have seen the beauty of its carvings.

CONTROL

Being ill often makes us feel desperately out of control. Today's medical system demands hypervigilance as doctors spend so little time with patients and nurses are overwhelmed, overworked, and underpaid. It feels like a fatal mistake may be right around the corner, and if we remove our attention and support for even a second, our loved one could disappear.

This kind of pressure can easily turn us into "control freaks," as we are revved up with inhuman vigilance to make sure everything is done correctly. When our loved one dies, that state of control can continue into the funeral. After all, there are calls and decisions to be made as to the type of ceremony, including where and when.

Randi shared in her bereavement group about her husband's stay in the hospital. "There was so much to do and control," she said, "but now I see that it was just busyness. Ultimately, it was out of my hands, and the things I worried about made no difference in the end. But I had to be doing something."

This is like the stereotypical way we rush to boil water when a woman is giving birth. We don't need boiled water any longer, since sterilization is done these days in a high-tech way. But just as Randi described, it gives us something to do. However, when things begin to settle down, we are still left with the need to control, even when we don't recognize it.

Have you found yourself obsessing over things after a death in the family? A mother and daughter were so caught up in control when the man of the house was dying, they constantly fought with each other. They hadn't fought before, but now they couldn't agree on anything. Should they keep the room warm or cold? Should they take a nontraditional or Western approach? Even after he died, they kept fighting, this time over the raising of the grandkids. They each had gotten into the habit of controlling, and when their loved one passed away, they couldn't stop.

The truth is that they were fighting over lost control, so their arguing, as bad as it felt, was better than feeling the loss. Control covers painful feelings such as sadness, hurt, and anger. Many of us would prefer to fight it out rather than feel grief, loss, and seemingly inconsolable pain.

But control feels empty and harsh as it covers up the more vulnerable sensations underneath. Control gives the illusion of safety and helps us think we are holding everything together, but an illusion is all it is. And breaking it is a daunting task. In the movie *Broadcast News,* Holly Hunter played a very controlling news producer. In one scene she is confronted about her controlling behavior by her boss, who says sarcastically, "It must be great to always be right."

Her unexpected answer? "No, it's hell."

Trying to control the uncontrollable ultimately becomes a living hell, and grief has a way of amplifying everything and making people slaves to their own behavior. No one at Gerald's bakery felt they could do anything right after he lost his wife. Nothing was being handled properly, the cakes didn't taste as good as usual, the deliveries went out slower, and there was dissension among the previously happy employees. Pam, who had worked with Gerald for years, approached the man's mother. "We're doing everything the same way we've done it for years," she said, "but Gerald feels like nothing we do is right. We got things running smoothly when he was with his wife in the hospital for a month, but now that he's trying to control everything, he sees us as inadequate and incompetent."

Gerald's mother took her son aside and said, "If you get

everything perfect at work, it won't bring her back. The world is not perfect, and you can't fix your grief by obsessing over things that don't need fixing. Your staff knows what they're doing."

She continued, "Do you remember how clean the house was after your father died and what a neat person I became? Nothing was in its right place, and I kept rearranging the furniture because I was trying to fix something that wasn't fixable. One day, I found you and your sister crying. Your sister said to me, 'Mommy, we can't make everything perfect.' In that moment I realized what I was doing."

Gerald reluctantly realized that his mother was right. His need to control was getting him nowhere and was making work harder for everyone else. Things weren't perfect, and they could never go back to the way they were before his wife died. He let go of overcontrolling his staff and put his energy into some much-needed repairs on his house.

Grief can turn friends into controllers as well, as they try to end your grief so they can feel better. When Karen lost her best friend of ten years to liver disease, she was devastated. A few of her friends had planned a cruise to the Bahamas and they decided the best thing for Karen was to join them. They told her no ifs, ands, or buts, she was coming with them.

She didn't feel like joining them, but her friends would not take no for an answer. When her ship pulled up anchor and sailed off, Karen knew she had made a mistake. While her friends were having the time of their lives eating, drinking, and dancing, she walked the decks aimlessly, unable to stop thinking about her friend. She labeled the liner "The Ghost Ship" while her friends tried to drag her to banquets and activities. All she wanted to do was sit in silence, and when she got back home, she wished she had listened to her inner voice instead of allowing her friends to control her.

When Karen's friends tried to control her grief, she learned the hard way that grief travels with you, wherever you go.

But control doesn't always have to be negative. Walter's father, who was grieving the loss of his wife, complained about all the decisions he had to make. It was so hard for him to be on his own, he could barely decide what to have for dinner. Walter, who lived across the country, said, "Dad, why don't you come out here for a few months? When you get here, I promise you won't have a single decision. Just get on the plane." He sent his father a ticket, knowing he could cash it in if necessary. But his dad took the bait in the guise of not wanting to waste the ticket.

For the next three months, Walter made good on his promise. He lovingly controlled his father's every move, asking for his help in his construction business and keeping up the garden. In essence, taking control of his father's life was the greatest gift he could ever have offered as his father slowly healed his grief.

And so, whether it is perceived as helpful or intrusive, trying to stop someone from controlling others can be the ultimate controlling act.

Let your intuition guide you, since control can be like salt: a dab of it can make something a little better, but too much can spoil it completely.

FANTASY

"Moving Mom from Boston to Phoenix," says Beth, "was the best thing we ever did. And when the house next door came on the market at an affordable price, it was an unbelievable coincidence. Mom loves being next door to us. She says she loves waking up early and coming over and making coffee and breakfast for everyone. We feel like an old-fashioned close-knit family. The kids love having Grandma around, and she says they make her feel young again.

"Our biggest problem is the path that got worn on the lawn between our houses. I can't believe it's been five years since she moved here. She's actually thinking about taking a Spanish class with our nineteen-year-old. Life is so much richer with her . . ."

Beth's eyes welled up with tears. "That was the fantasy," she said. "I never dreamed I would be at her funeral only three months after she moved here."

We are never lacking a fantasy about how things should be. From our earliest memories we fantasize about our lives and how they will be, who will be with us, and how it will all turn out in the end. When we are grieving, it is hard to let go of the fantasies, especially when death has taken a loved one from us unexpectedly. Beth and her mother shared a fantasy about retirement. They made the plans and did the move; then her mother unexpectedly became ill. Now Beth lives with the fantasy of what might have been.

Beth not only has the loss of her mother to grieve, but she also needs to separately and simultaneously mourn the fantasy. Loss is so complex and complicated that at times we need to break it down into parts: the loss of Mother, Grandmother, friend, and the life that was left unlived. The fantasy left behind is part of that loss too and deserves its own grief. Grief feels even more overwhelming when all the parts and losses of it are dumped on us like crates of old belongings that we can't let go. But if we can separate out the parts and give each of them its due, they can feel like a warm, sad shower we take to cleanse our souls. In Beth's case, she needed to grieve her mother, but she also needed to grieve the fantasy of how they would live next to each other for a decade or two.

A few weeks after the funeral they put the house back on the market and it sold quickly. But the sale was not based on price alone. Beth requested to meet the potential buyers and told them what the house had meant to her. She was pleased that they were sensitive to her story, because she had vowed not to sell to anyone who did not exhibit compassionate feelings for her and her mother.

Before escrow closed, she brought an air mattress to the house that her mother had never really had a chance to occupy. She spent the night there, crying for the lost fantasy that the house represented.

When the new family took possession, Beth had let go enough to wish them well. Her choice to do a ritual that was not only about grieving her mother but grieving the house was a good one.

For Beth, mourning what never happened was tangible. In some cases, however, it is not so easy. When Jim's wife died, he had no plans to move, and yet he still had the fantasy of their retirement and their trips that never happened. But unlike Beth, he had no house in which to spend the night. How would Jim mourn a trip to Africa that they had planned for many years? Jim did not want to do this trip without his wife, and in a grief workshop he talked about being unable to mourn the trip that never was. When he asked for suggestions, the facilitator suggested he get to the roots of the idea. How did it come about?

Jim explained it was a number of events. He and his wife had liked the movie *Out of Africa* so much, they visited San Diego's Wild Animal Park and decided then and there that when they retired, they would go on a real African safari.

For Jim, getting to the roots of the idea became the way to separate and mourn the retirement fantasy. He rented *Out of Africa,* watched it alone, and cried the whole way through. In a few weeks, he took a solitary day trip to San Diego's Wild Animal

Park. He felt that these rituals provided a tangible way to grieve the adventure that might have been.

We can also get lulled into fantasy thinking that is not realistic, such as how we could have changed the outcome: "If I had been with him, I could have stopped the car accident." The truth is that in most cases the death would have happened anyway. But in our fantasy of changing things, we get to connect with our loved one, see them alive in our mind, and bargain that they might temporarily come alive again.

We also rewrite the past in smaller ways concerning our loved ones. We idealize what was and who our loved one was. Joseph and Sophie had had a challenging relationship. Joseph never really found the career success he wanted, which had caused them to move a lot, leaving Sophie feeling uprooted most of the time. She also had health problems that caused her to have bad days and worse days, living with kidney disease that wreaked havoc if she didn't monitor her health and diet closely. All this, mixed with his temper and her selfishness, only worsened with her illness. She would often feel insecure and imagined that Joseph was unfaithful.

At first he tried to convince her that it was not true, but he grew tired of the accusations and began to resent her. They spent more time arguing than talking, but as her health failed, he stood fast by her side. After she died, in his grief, he began to reconstruct their life together as one in which Sophie could do no wrong. He saw her as never having been anything less than perfect and loving, and in his mind he created a powerful fantasy about who she was. He, like so many others before him, idealized her in death with a marriage they never had in life.

People often change reality to fantasy after death. Some of this is cultural. We are taught never to speak ill of the dead, and we feel guilty for even remembering the mistakes they made. We often idealize the person we lost to subconsciously convey the enormity of what is gone. The greater the person, we think, the more others will understand all that we have lost.

Sometimes we just purify the past to make it more palatable. We don't want to air our mistakes, especially in loss. The downside to all this is that we may miss mourning the total person and all that they were, good and bad, light and dark.

STRENGTH

"Be strong." These two little words are often declared to those in grief. Men hear them more often than women, and surviving parents are told, "Be strong for the sake of the children."

Jennifer heard those words after her husband died. "My loss was so bad," she said, "I never knew how to take those words of advice. Did people think I wasn't supposed to cry in front of the kids? I didn't, just because someone told me not to. But I began to get angry, as if they were telling me I was grieving wrong. I didn't want to have to be strong. My heart was too shattered to put on airs. And yet I did. I did it for the kids, I thought."

We are often told to be strong by people with good intentions. "Take it like a man," the message tells us. "You're showing too much emotion. Don't be a wimp." As if we shouldn't be affected by death. But sometimes our "be strong" means not being human.

That kind of bravery belongs to heroes who need to act in the face of danger. But bravery does not mean being unfeeling. In our society it has become confused with keeping a stiff upper lip. The bottom line is that strength can certainly be channeled into loss, but it can also violate it.

A senior in high school was playing on the school football team when his mother died. The very next day, the rival school was coming to play them in the big game, and the teenager was shattered. His coach said, "Play for your mom, be strong, be brave, go win it for her."

That sounded like a great movie plot, but the team was on a losing streak and they lost that day too. Years later the young man talked about how violated he had felt. "The last place I wanted to be was on a football field, but I didn't know what else to do." In his case, there were no points for not grieving and none for being brave.

There are situations, however, that go the other way when someone consciously directs his grief into the game to honor a loved one. But even then it often sends a message that to grieve well, you get up and get on with it. The problem with that premise is that in order to be strong, one has to shut down the emotions.

Why do people tell us to be strong? Maybe because they hear it in the movies in such a motivational way, it seems that it does no harm or causes no interference in the grieving process. And then, people are always more comfortable when the grieving person does not give off the sense that he or she is falling apart. If the grieving person doesn't cry and express too many emotions, we won't feel too much either. The truth is that pain can be contagious. You can't be around someone in deep sadness and not feel it, so if we put a lid on the grieving person's emotions, we won't have to deal with them ourselves.

But at what cost do we camouflage our grief? When we shelve our pain, it doesn't go away. Rather, it festers in a myriad of ways. We need to understand that strength and grief fit together. We must be strong to handle grief, and in the end, grief brings out strengths we never knew we had.

Jennifer was told to be strong for her children when her husband died. Today she wonders about the message her dry eyes implied. Did her children think she didn't care? "What if I *did* cry in front of the kids? What if I modeled grief for them in that way? I could have said, 'Mommy is sad and crying because Daddy has died.' I could have reassured them that I was still strong enough to be there for them and take care of them." Children need to know that strong people cry when loved ones die and that does not hamper their ability to go on with life. Jennifer feels she missed an opportunity to share her loss instead of demonstrating a façade of false strength.

Strength in grief shows up in many different ways. Wanda, grieving the loss of her twin brother, Dwayne, to cancer, was devastated by his absence. A month into her loss, a friend, Gail, came to visit and was horrified to see Wanda in her pajamas, still sobbing uncontrollably.

"You have to be strong," Gail told her distraught friend. "It's Saturday. Let's go shopping. You need to get back out there. It's been a whole month. You can't work all week and cry all weekend. What kind of a life is that?"

Wanda looked at her friend through her tears and asked, "What's so strong about going to the mall? Gail, the real question is, do you have the strength to sit here with me in my sorrow?"

Wanda had the strength to say what others only wish they'd said. All too often, someone chooses shopping or fishing to placate a friend or to avoid their own pain. Most of us would do just about anything rather than sit with someone in grief. But grief must be fully experienced to provide the healing on the other side. The only way out is through it, so you can put it off but you can't skip it. To delay it is to live with grief sitting mildly in the background, or for some, not so mildly.

When the pain and sadness hit, you can do what Wanda was attempting to do. Just sit with it. If you feel sad, let yourself feel that sadness. Do the same with anger and disappointment. If you need to cry all day long, do it. The only thing to avoid is repressing the hurt or artificially trying to bring it on when it isn't raw enough to express. What we are trying to achieve here is to feel the pain and then feel the release that follows it.

Be aware that when grief hits in all of its power, we instinctually try to resist the sense of overwhelm. But resistance to pain only serves to amplify it. Try sinking into it and feel it become more spacious. Allow it to wash over you and feel the strength return to your body and your mind. When you surrender to grief, you will discover that you are so much stronger than you ever imagined. Peace lies at the center of the pain, and although it will hurt, you *will* move through it a lot faster than if you distracted yourself with external outings.

Wanda's instincts told her exactly what she needed and she followed them, even when her friend disagreed. Although there are times when the mind needs a rest and a little distraction can be a good thing, one of the greatest injustices we can do to a friend is try to pull them out of grief before they're ready. You just can't look to anyone else to tell you when your sadness will be over. It may be a month, a year, two years, or a lot longer. Only you will know when your loss is integrated and it's time to come out and rejoin the world.

We often have residual feelings from our loved one's death. We think about what strength meant to them and to us. During many rounds with an illness, we and our loved ones may often have heard the battle cry, "Be strong and fight the disease!"

We are sure that strong people can beat it. She will make it. Cancer is no match for a strong husband or a fiercely determined wife. The message is that strength is life and death is weakness.

So what are we left with when our loved one dies—weakness? Does it mean they weren't strong enough to make it? Did they succumb? Did they lose the battle? We often are left believing that someone was too weak to fight, so they "succumbed." Does this mean that they lost and the illness won?

Are we all destined to die as failures?

Just as a woman must be strong enough to give birth, we must have a great deal of strength to die. Some spiritual systems believe that we give our permission to be born into the world, and we give our permission to die.

Over many years of experience in the death and dying field, we have seen the struggle that ensues when a soul is attempting to leave a body. And then there comes that quiet moment of surrender, when strength is about letting go rather than holding on. As you look back at the death, you may see things differently in retrospect. Your loved one was powerful to get through all that he or she did when battling the disease. And they were even more powerful when they finally let go into the unknown, dying into strength, not weakness.

When all is said and done, facing a loss takes an enormous amount of strength and determination that gives meaning to our loss and honors our loved one.

AFTERLIFE

Jan and Jeffrey had been married for ten years. Jeffrey jokes, "We were more married than anyone I've ever known. In fact, it seems like we were married from the first day we met."

One day while they were taking a cruise, Jan felt a pain in her hip when she was exercising. She figured it was a pulled muscle—no big deal—and she continued exercising. When they arrived back home and got settled in, it was a Saturday night and Jan insisted, "Let's go to the early church service."

"We go every week, and we just got home," Jeffrey said, surprised at Jan's urgency. "I'm sure we could miss one service."

When the pain of Jan's pulled leg muscle didn't go away, she became engrossed in reading about how after the 9/11 tragedy, people were deep in faith and spent lots of time praying. It seemed that her pain medication was doing nothing, and while she waited to return to the doctor, she started reading as much religious material as she could get her hands on. She became fascinated with stories of people who had died, and one day she told her husband, "Jeffrey, I know I'm going to die because my grandmother came to me and said, 'You will come be with us soon.'"

Jan assured Jeffrey that she wasn't scared, because she had loved her grandmother so much and it was actually comforting.

Jeffrey laughed it off, telling her, "People have visitations on their deathbed, not after a pulled muscle at the gym."

Jan insisted that she felt God telling her it was okay to die. "That's why I go to church so much these days," she explained to Jeffrey, "to hear that it's okay to die. I need to hear it over and over again."

Jeffrey said he simultaneously dismissed her thoughts of dying and feared they were true, especially since she had a doctor's visit coming up because the pain hadn't gone away. Over the next few weeks, Jeffrey wanted Jan to see a psychiatrist about her belief that she was dying.

"I'm sorry, Jeff," she said, "but it's true. I'm going to die. Why else would I be spending so much time in my dreams visiting with deceased family members and friends? I don't want to go, Jeff, but I know it's my time."

After her next medical workup, she was diagnosed with lung

cancer that had metastasized to her bones. The doctors told her that it had already advanced so far, there wasn't much she could do, that she probably had had it for many years. The fact that she was a young nonsmoker had placed her in a low risk category for cancer, so it was unlikely she'd have found out sooner.

For the next month, Jan did her best to comfort Jeffrey. "They came to help me, to get me ready," she said. "God and I knew long before the doctors did, and I know that it's going to be okay when I die. I really hope you can find a way to be reassured that we continue on after death and I'll be there for you when it's your time. I want you to live a full life after I am gone and to know that wherever I go, I'm not alone."

After she died, Jeffrey understood it wasn't that Jan had been attracted to death and religion for the last year of her life; rather, they had come to her to help.

Visitations are a commonly reported afterlife phenomenon. For example, a dying patient has a vision of her mother, who has been dead for twenty years. Her mother tells her that everything will be okay and she will be waiting for her. These things happen a great deal, but modern medicine tries to explain them away, calling them hallucinations brought on by pain medication, or wishful thinking.

But why is the concept of visitation so hard to believe? Imagine that you're a parent who had loved and cared for your child. You kept her fed, healthy, and safe while she was growing up. You helped her when she skinned her knee, when she was afraid of the dark, when she felt insecure about high school. You shared her excitement and fears of college, marriage, and becoming a parent herself.

Now go forward sixty to eighty years into the future. You've been dead for decades, and your daughter, the same one you helped through all her scary moments in life, is now dying herself. Wouldn't you go meet her if you could? As the veil between life and death is lifting, wouldn't you want to reassure her she's going be okay and you're still there for her? When you think about it that way, maybe it doesn't sound quite as far-fetched. Many people believe that when they die, everyone they have ever loved and known will be there to greet them in death. That is why they believe no one actually dies alone.

After death, you will also experience a review of your life. You will review it not in the first person, not as you experienced it in life. But you will review it from the perspective of how everyone else experienced you. You will feel all the consequences of your actions. You will know all the pain and more importantly all the love and kindness that others felt from you. This will be not a punitive experience but a learning one. You will see how far you have grown in your life and whether you have more lessons to learn. You will be asked how much did you love and how much service did you do for mankind.

Whatever the truth about life after death, we are certain that death does not exist as we imagine it. If you feel your loved one's presence, do not doubt it. They still exist. Birth is not a beginning and death is not an ending. They are merely points on a continuum. Death does not exist in its usually traditional form as an "ending to all." We are not suggesting that when you lose your loved one, you can skip the terrible pain of loss and separation, but we believe with all our hearts that even in death, our loved one still exists.

On the other hand, there are many in our society who believe that when you die, that is it. There is nothing else, and your energy lives on only in those around you. If this is true, then our loved ones live on in us in an even more tangible way than we thought.

Many societies believe that the body is just a coat, a suit of clothes that we wear during this lifetime. You may have sat by someone's body after they died and have seen that this was a shell, a cocoon left behind. It was not your loved one anymore. And you could feel this absence of their spirit, their energy. Life continues beyond the death of a physical body. It is only the warmth and calm of a transformation of a cocoon to a butterfly. You don't see the butterfly, but you feel the relief of knowing that your loved one is no longer in pain, no longer hooked up to tubes and sick in a bed; they are no longer diseased. Your loved one is now free of all that.

Our beliefs in the afterlife play a role in how we grieve, the impact being left to each individual. Questioning it is nothing new. Since the beginning of time, human beings have been concerned with what happens after we die: Where is our loved one now? We thought he was his body, but his body is finished and we can still feel him in our hearts. Exactly when and how did he leave? Even in the moments before death and sometimes for hours or days, we see the body barely breathing, and somehow we know our loved one is no longer inhabiting it.

"I can just feel he's not here anymore." We have heard this many times, this sense that the loved one was already absent from his body when he died. Families sit in a circle around a body for days on end, but when their loved one dies, they unconsciously remove their focus from the body. They may suddenly realize they are no longer giving attention to their loved one's body the way they were before. They must know that on some level, their loved one's energy is no longer pulling or attracting their attention. The energy has been disbanded.

At the moment of death, we assume that our loved one is in the midst of separating the mortal from the immortal. She is leaving behind the temporary house, her body, and moving into the depth of the spirit and the soul—what many call the "Immortal

Self." It has been reported that at the moment of death, we experience a total absence of panic, fear, or anxiety. We feel the physical wholeness that was missing, like an amputee feeling her severed leg, or a deaf person hearing beautiful music.

Our belief in the afterlife dictates how we feel about someone's dying. If you believe she will go to heaven, you may be sad she's gone but reassured that she is happy in heaven. If you believe there is nothing after death, you can derive reassurance that she is no longer suffering. If you believe in reincarnation, you may wonder who she will be next. When will they be born? If you believe in heaven, you will be relieved if she led a good life.

Some feel that our loved ones live on, but on another plane of existence. They may believe a loved one is around but is now transmitting signals, like radio or TV that we in our limited physical world can't pick up. And yet we long to. We may try to contact the dead, to speak to them and pierce the veil between life and death. It is futile to debate the reality of this, for it is beyond our knowing.

In loss we are looking and longing for connection. The longing for that exploration should be stopped and questioned only if you believe it is being exploited by someone for unscrupulous reasons. If someone says they have experienced it, the only question that is important is, "Were you comforted?"

Whatever you believe, your grief will be tied to how you feel about the afterlife. You may not have any belief about the afterlife but just feel the loss of your loved one here. For some, the afterlife is of no concern. They are just feeling the pain here on earth.

A young boy, Johnny, always passed his church on his way to school. Although he didn't go in, each day he opened the door to the church and said, "God, it's me, Johnny." Then he smiled, closed the door, and went on his way to school.

As he became older, he continued to stick his head in churches for a minute and say, "God, it's me, Johnny." When his tenth grade class went on a trip to London during the summer, he opened every unlocked church door and announced his presence to God, smiling as if he was catching him off guard by being in London.

A few years later when he was a high school senior, Johnny was killed in a car accident. But the second before he died, Johnny heard a voice that said, "Johnny, it's me, God."

This story was told by a hospice and palliative care nurse who heard it from a nun in Catholic school. It continues to be passed on with a few changes here and there, but it comforts those who hear it with a promise of an afterlife. It seems that whether we believe in heaven, God, reincarnation, or white light, we are comforted by the sense that there is a hereafter, that we are more than bodies and have more than one mortal life with a beginning, a middle, and an end.

The dying experience is similar to that of birth, just as the growth of the caterpillar is the natural step toward emergence of the butterfly. Just as we cannot hear a dog whistle, which sounds at a frequency too high for the human ear, we cannot hear our loved one broadcasting on a channel whose frequency is beyond our ears' capabilities. But that doesn't mean that our loved one can't hear us. A ship exists on the ocean, even if it sails out beyond the limits of our sight. The people in the ship have not vanished; they are simply moving to another shore.

In the same way, death can be viewed as a transition to a higher state of consciousness where you continue to perceive, understand, and grow. The only thing you lose is something that you don't need anymore, your physical body. It's like putting away your winter coat when spring comes. You lose something that you don't need anymore, something that may have been sick, old, and no longer in working order. That understanding may leave little comfort in the immediate moment, but in the long run, it helps to know that somewhere, somehow, our loved one still exists and we will see them again.

The trouble is that in grief, a moment feels like a year and a year feels like an eternity. It has to be easier for the one who has moved into the next reality, where there is no time, even if we see ourselves as a moment behind. Frank and Margaret had been married for fifty wonderful years, over which time they were mostly inseparable. When Margaret became terminally ill, she said, "I can accept this illness. I can accept the reality that I'm going to die. The hardest thing for me to accept is that I'm going to be without Frank."

As Margaret's disease progressed, she was more and more disturbed by the prospect of this ultimate separation. Hours before she died, she turned to Frank, who was sitting at her bedside. Her mind was clear and alert, for she had not taken any medications. She said, "I'm going to be leaving soon. And it's finally okay."

"What made it okay for you?" he asked.

She replied, "I've just been told I'm going to a place where you already are."

Is it possible that Frank was simultaneously sitting in the hospital room and waiting for his beloved wife in heaven? Perhaps the question revolves around our perception of time. For Frank, who lives and breathes in earth time, it may be five, ten, or twenty years before he sees Margaret again. But if she's going to a place where there is no time, it may seem that he arrives a second behind her.

There is no doubt that is easier for our loved ones who have died, since there is no time for them. We, on the other hand, are stuck in time, and for us in grief that moment may feel like forever.

Children have no agendas when it comes to the afterlife, which is probably why we hear so many cases in which dying children validate an afterlife. A twelve-year-old child who came back from a near-death experience decided not to tell her mother that dying in a car accident was a beautiful experience. She didn't want to hurt her mother's feelings by telling her that she had been happy in a place greater than her home.

She had a need to talk about it, though, so she told her father that dying was a beautiful experience and she had not wanted to come back. In fact, not only was it an experience of light and openheartedness, she had been amazed to meet with someone who said he was her brother, who told her she was going to be fine. "He loved me so much," she said, "and he loved you and Mom, too. How could I have seen someone who said he was my brother? I don't have a brother."

Her father began to cry. "You did have a brother, but he died before you were born," her dad said. "We wanted to tell you when you got older."

We often make the mistake of thinking all communication ends at death. Why do we find nothing unusual about talking to an unborn child in utero, but if we talk to the deceased, people might think we're crazy? The truth is that even after death, it's never too late to say you're sorry or how much you loved your spouse or mother or friend. The truth is that you can finish "unfinished business" even if you've held on to it for ten, twenty years or even more.

When we die, we will be surprised that not only those who loved us the most will be waiting, but there will also be many others. Ancestors, and strangers whose lives we touched and never knew it. It's easy to imagine that when we die all our old friends will gather to welcome us to the next world.

Many people believe in reincarnation, that their soul leaves the body and is reborn in another one. It is said that we are reincarnated with the same people over and over, that we come into this world with lessons to learn in the midst of others who have the same task.

We are a society that demands proof for most things, but some things simply cannot be proved. For example, if a friend asked you to touch your nose, you could do that and you would both agree that it was done. It would be the same result if your friend asked you to touch your chin. But if you were asked to touch the love you feel for your child or your parent, what would you touch?

We will all wonder what the afterlife is and what it will be like. Some think the importance lies in the answer. But just the question is enough. What does seem to be important is that the bereaved are comforted by the thought and feeling that their loved one still exists somehow.

3. The Outer World of Grief

ANNIVERSARIES

Mourning is the external part of loss. It is the actions we take, the rituals and the customs. Grief is the internal part of loss, how we feel. The internal work of grief is a process, a journey. It does not end on a certain day or date. It is as individual as each of us. In your first year you have mourned and grieved. Life and grief are made up of good days and bad days.

We don't realize how many anniversaries there are in life until after a loss. We are aware that there will be anniversaries of the day our loved one died, but we forget the celebrations and/or remembrances of birth, marriages, that first date, and the millions of things in between. Whatever happiness they once brought, now they bring memories of deep loss. Every symbol of the anniversary of a death matters to us: the one-month anniversary, six months, a year.

People will not remind you of the date, as if you could forget, because they don't know what to say. You don't know what to say yourself, because after a death occurs, all those anniversaries take on new and heightened meanings. Now you have to spend them without the person who made them celebratory. Joy is replaced on those days now by the feeling of loss.

Friends often will avoid calling to say, "It's thirty days (or three months or a year) and I wanted to give you a call, but I was too afraid of hurting you." If you want others to feel comfortable talking about it, you'll have to give them a signal that you are aware of the date. Silly as that is, it is one of those things in our society that we fear the most. It's hard to call a widow and say, "I'm so sorry your husband has been gone for six months now." A friend fears that if they called to console you, you might say, "I was having a good day. I actually forgot. But now you brought back the pain."

It is not likely that anyone would get mad at a friend for calling to say they were thinking about your loss, but we have heard this concern over and over. Even if the person did forget, they usually haven't forgotten subconsciously, because our bodies remember our feelings. We see this in children in foster homes. Social workers will tell you when a child will often have a problem: the same time of year they were put into the foster system or the same day their parents died. Children have a remarkably tough time on specific days. The shocking thing about this phenomenon is that it happens in children too young to know the calendar yet.

We are no different as adults. Roxanne was late for work. She hadn't slept well, she was making lots of mistakes at work, and she was edgy and irritable. She was sure it was the lack of sleep. Then it hit her, when a coworker happened to ask the date. "It's June twenty-first," she said, stumbling over the words as she realized that had been her wedding anniversary.

There are many times we may remember the date of a friend's loss because it was four days before our birthday, and we think we should call. If the person is not aware of the date, they will usually say, "No wonder I felt so sad today," or "That's why I was having such a hard day." Most often will they thank their friend for remembering and caring.

Maria and Paul were looking for the right time in their schedules to spend two weeks together in France. They decided to take the trip just before the holiday season, but they would miss Maria's mother's birthday. One week before their trip, they took Patricia (Maria's mother) out to celebrate her sixty-fourth birthday.

When they were in France on the actual day of Patricia's birthday, they thought about her all day long. "Hey," said Maria, "let's a have birthday dinner tonight in my mom's honor." That night they had a great time telling stories about her and joking about how she probably wasn't really sixty-four; she kept her real age a secret.

When they returned from the trip and told Patricia how they had celebrated her birthday, she loved the idea of the dinner in her absence. She joked with her friends about how her family had her birthday dinner in France, often leaving out the part that she wasn't there. All the relatives knew, but they played along with the wonderful charade of the birthday dinner in France.

The next summer, Patricia was furious when she found out her house had been broken into. That evening she was at the police station recounting the story and suddenly had a massive heart attack. She did not survive.

When the next Christmas arrived, after Patricia's death, Paul and Maria were at a loss as to how they would ever get through the holidays. Christmas might be okay, since their children would keep them busy, but how would they celebrate Patricia's birthday, which came at the same time?

They thought back to the celebrations that they had in the past, which were all similar except for the preceding year when they had been in France, so they decided to have a party that year for Patricia's birthday even though Patricia would be absent.

Just as they did the year before, they toasted her and told stories. "We would never have considered a birthday dinner after my mom had died," Maria told her friends, "but I knew how much she loved us gathering in her honor and everyone talking about her." The cousins came and they had a big dinner, which made it feel real to Maria. "All the relatives and siblings were there," she recalls, "and so were the grandkids. We all had a wonderful night reminiscing and proposing toasts."

She told her coworkers the next day, "It seemed like the perfect thing to do. It would have been a sad, empty event, but since we did it the year before, we knew Mom would love the idea of it."

In Maria's case, her family decided it was easier for them to celebrate her birthday than to not do anything. But everyone is different. What matters is that you spend anniversaries doing something that comforts you. For some, the pain is so great that working and keeping busy is best. Others will want to take some time with friends to talk about their feelings and their great loss. Some may want to reminisce privately on their own.

When the first year and other yearly anniversaries come, you may want to do more. On yearly anniversaries, especially the first, you may want to commemorate your loss. Find your own way to honor your loved one's memory. It is an occasion that may bring up your greatest sadness along with some of your best memories. It deserves its spot in your heart. Just do what feels right for you. Attend a service, visit your loved one's grave, or just talk to friends and family. Honor the love and the memories left behind.

Brenda was missing her husband, Douglas, terribly when the first anniversary of his death approached. She thought she would light a candle in his honor, but she knew she needed more, so she invited a few friends over on the anniversary of the night he died. She also sent an e-mail to friends who lived out of town and a few who were out of the country, asking for e-mails about memories of Douglas.

When the night arrived, she had four of Douglas's close friends over, and one by one, each told a story about Douglas and then read three e-mails. Then they lit a candle and said, "I light this candle in remembrance of you, Douglas, and I give thanks for knowing you." After they each had a turn, they went out to dinner at Douglas's favorite restaurant.

Brenda said it was perfect. "It symbolized for me how his body is gone," she said, "but the connection is never gone. It was everything: head, heart, and the eternal. Early in the night we were more serious in our sadness and gratitude, and after we had voiced our thoughts and read the e-mails we had a great night out. The dinner was light, fun, and unexpected."

Brenda found a way to honor Douglas and remember his anniversary. Anniversaries may also be a time to honor yourself for having strength and courage. A year ago or years ago you were a different person. The person you were is forever changed.

A part of the old you died with your loved one. And a part of your loved one lives on in the new you.

SEX

Judith, a woman in her late sixties, said that her marriage had almost ended in divorce thirty-five years ago. She revealed how on the day her son died from cancer, seven hours later to be exact, her husband wanted to have sex with her.

"I was devastated by the loss and was extremely insulted by his selfishness and insensitivity. How could my husband think of something as enjoyable as sex, when I wasn't sure life would ever be enjoyable again? It was beyond my comprehension. But luckily for us, we had a strong marriage that withstood my husband's request, which I thought was completely inappropriate. I knew he loved our son as much as I did, so I could never quite comprehend his feeling sexual at a time like that."

Years later her husband shared what he could not articulate at the time. "It wasn't really sex I was after," he told her. "I was lost after our son died. I felt not only the emptiness in our family but also an emptiness in my soul. I needed to be held so I could feel like I was connected, that we were joined together. Sex was the only way I knew how to tap into those feelings."

Judith learned what we rarely speak about and usually do not put into print: daring to talk about sex in the context of grief has long been taboo—even with a person's closest friends. If it comes up at all, it's usually behind a counselor's closed doors. Even then the discussion is almost always vague. But for us not to discuss it in this book would be to deny the real feelings and events that sometimes happen after a loss.

Men and women experience sex and grief differently, but we will speak in generalities. As in Judith's case, men don't always know how to say, "I feel alone and I need to be held." Women are much more able to ask for tactile support than men, which made Judith's husband's request for sex seem like an insult to the memory of their deceased son. But it isn't so.

Sex is a part of life, so it is also a part of grief. When a husband or wife or lover dies, there is a loss of sex as well. You may have wonderful memories of lovemaking, which are not so easily discussed with friends. Maybe you want to have sex right away, and maybe you'll never want it again as long as you live. For some, the avoidance of sex may pass in time, and for others sex will remain a memory.

One thing is sure: if sex was part of the relationship, it will be part of the grief. When a partner dies, we tend to consciously or unconsciously assign their roles to other people or to ourselves. He handled the finances; now you do. He handled the house repairs; now you hire someone. She cared for the children; now you get help from Grandma and day care. But what is to be done with the natural desire for sex that may eventually reappear? It is a role that is not so easily reassigned.

In the early days or months—or years—of grief, the idea of sex may not even cross your mind. But when it does, how do you interpret it—as a natural desire returning? Do you see it for what it really is, or are you clouded with thoughts of betrayal and upset? Sex represented not only a physical act but an emotional intimacy that you two shared. It was most likely a very important part of your relationship. Because of this, you miss not only your lover but also the sexual part of yourself—the part that lives on after your lover has died. The part that still has a primal need for connection.

When sexual feelings arise after a death, it's easy to judge yourself. How could you have these feelings without your loved one? How *dare* you? It's as if everyone assumes that someone with a loss should never experience normal feelings and desires again. Nevertheless, you do, only this time without your loved one, which seems like a kind of posthumous infidelity. Recognize these feelings as healthy and normal. Do not denounce sex simply because you think you should. Do you denounce food because you always ate with your loved one?

When Jamie was in her junior year of college, her father fell ill. She told her boyfriend, Mark, that she needed to go back home to be with her family. They had been casually dating for about a year, and he supported her returning home. A week after she arrived at her family home, her father passed away, and after the funeral she returned to college. Mark dropped by her dorm with flowers to console her, but he was surprised to find that she wanted to have sex.

He hesitated, knowing she was a virgin. "Are you sure?" he asked. "You always said you wanted to wait till your wedding night."

To her own amazement, she said, "I'm sure." As they began to kiss, he was surprised at the depth of her intensity, but he went with it. When it was over, it hit him that their lovemaking had been driven by her grief.

They remained friends and years later, when they met for lunch to catch up, she brought up their encounter following her father's death. "When I came back from the funeral," she said, "I was covered in death. I needed to feel the intensity of life, and sex was the only way I thought I could get there."

He was thoughtful for a moment. Then he said, "I always wonder if I should have tried harder to say no. I knew you had a romantic picture for your first time."

"There was no way you could have talked me out of it," she reassured him.

Barbara lost her husband to cancer after three years of radiation, chemo, and pain medication. All of her focus had been on her husband's survival. When a friend called four months after his death to see if she wanted to attend their twentieth high school reunion, Barbara agreed to tag along. Her friend would arrange the logistics and do the driving; all Barbara needed to do was pack and get in the car. Barbara's friend felt the distraction of her old friends would be a good thing.

Barbara was surprised when she ran into her old prom date, Ron, and even more surprised when they danced together and she felt sexually attracted to him once again. After a few glasses of wine at the bar, it was closing time, but she and Ron were enjoying reminiscing so much, they decided to continue in his room. The next thing they knew, they were kissing and making love.

In the morning when she returned to her room to shower and change, she felt enormously guilty. She judged herself, thinking it was too soon to feel sexual again, but then she realized that it had been close to four years since she'd had sex, because her husband had been so ill.

Whether it's four years or four months, having sex again is complicated. The "right time" depends on the person, the relationship, and what feels okay inside. Like Barbara, many people forget to factor in the time they spent nursing their loved one as they recall the length of celibacy, and for everyone it's different. For Barbara, the issue arose after her husband's death. For others dealing with long-term illness, the temptation to have sex outside the relationship during the partner's illness can be compelling and often very difficult to handle.

Joseph had been a loving husband for ten years when Kelly, his wife, was tragically killed in a car accident. An attorney who specialized in trusts, estates, and wills, Kelly had made certain that she and her husband had completed the advance directives. She had talked openly about what would happen if one of them died, saying she hoped he would use the life he had left. She mentioned a widow she knew, a coworker, whose husband had died prematurely. "If something ever happens to me," she told Joseph, "I want you to remarry." Joseph had agreed, but as he entered his second year of grief, although he could imagine someday marrying again, the idea of sex still felt like cheating.

For Joseph, as for many others, rejoining the living is a series of uncomfortable steps: dating, sex, and maybe love. Luckily he had his wife's words to fall back on, and they tenderly reminded him that he was not betraying her. But more often than not, people don't have that kind of reassurance. When we're in love, we don't want to think about loss.

Some people go back in their minds or hearts or even to their loved one's grave and ask for permission to continue with life. That usually contains the unspoken permission to date again, have sex again, and love again.

You'll have to trust yourself to know when and where to get back into a relationship again. But expect some difficulty and awkwardness at first. Hopefully your new partner will be understanding, or at the very least, you will understand your own journey and figure out how to maneuver it.

For example, if you and your loved one visited Hawaii often, going there with someone else will obviously trigger grief and guilt. So why do you ever imagine you could have sex again and not think about your lost love? It can't happen without old thoughts, but with compassion and patience, you can begin again. You can finally understand this shadow of grief and the courage it takes to go on living and loving.

During grief, sex means different things to different people. Some need to have sex soon after the loss; some decide to do it much later; and some do it when it just feels like it is time. Some use sex early on to escape the feelings of pain, since it can be distracting and numbing and help us escape grieving. Others consider it the perfect antidote to death. After all, sex is about life, the opposite of death.

Simon came home exhausted after being with his sick mother, who, despite the best efforts of the doctors, had just died of pneumonia. "When you lose your last parent," he said, "your current family becomes all you have in the world, and your spouse is even more important. When I arrived home I had a stronger than usual need to connect to Kim. The moment I walked in the door I fell into her arms. I brought my suitcase in the bedroom and she followed. I lay down on the bed and held her. Then when I kissed her she pulled back and said, 'You want to have sex?'

"Yes," I told her, "but not for the sake of sex. I feel like an orphan, like I don't have anywhere in the world to go but to you. I need to be with you to feel like I'm a part of something."

Kim did not understand and she said quite harshly, "You need to get your mind out of the gutter and do some crying."

Simon said later that he did not feel she had rejected only sex. "I felt like she was not there for me," he said. "She showed lack of sensitivity, and I couldn't explain to her that I needed to feel oneness because I felt so alone."

It can be hard to explain to your spouse that when a door closes, there's a sense that you have no place to go. The bonding that happens in sex can be comforting at such times because for many people, closeness and sexuality are bound together. Sex can reaffirm a connection quickly, and when it does, it's not about sex; it's about the closeness that sex makes possible.

In Simon's case it was not about fun and pleasure but rather about melting boundaries. After you experience the loss of a loved one, a solid boundary suddenly stands before you. It feels as if you've hit a hard wall, and you need to find some softness in your life. Death is the breaking of a connection, while sex can be the establishing of one.

We would suggest, however, that seeking counseling or a bereavement group is usually a better choice than seeking sex right away in order to sort out your feelings. Know that the grief will lie in wait until you are ready to deal with it. But we live in the real world, and we do not have grief counselors at our beck and call whenever the pain becomes unbearable. The bottom line is that we are human beings and we do the best we can.

YOUR BODY AND YOUR HEALTH

Donna sat by her husband's bed day in and day out as he lay in the hospital room on the oncology floor. She was consumed with making sure he had the best care, food if he was hungry, fresh water and ice chips and pain relief. She left his side only to go to the bathroom or go into the lobby to update relatives.

The nurses and her family were concerned, but not about Donna's husband. He was comfortable. They were concerned about Donna, who was pale with dark circles under her red and swollen eyes. She often had a stiff neck from sleeping in the chair. Unless someone asked her when her last meal was, she easily forgot to eat. When she remembered, usually late at night, her meals often came from the vending machines in the hallways. But no one could find fault in her weariness or meals of cheddar cheese crackers and Cokes because they knew her presence meant the world to her husband—and to Donna.

When Byron died, Donna was in a shockingly haggard state. But she had to kick into high gear for the wake and funeral. Despite her exhaustion, she made all the decisions about the funeral, the reception, and Byron's burial. She did her best to look good but even after she was freshly showered, with hair and makeup in place, everyone talked about how this loss had added ten years to Donna.

This is often the state we reach in grief. Remember, this is a very trying time. You have been through so much. Your body is worn down from all it has been through, all it has felt, and all you have seen. Now your body needs time to rest and rejuvenate, even though you may not want to or care. As much as your body may need your attention, it's natural to feel the pointlessness of taking care of yourself. After all, the only person you really cared about is gone.

How do you enter this new world of loss in which you find yourself? How do you go from "no time for meals" to "all the time in the world to eat"—especially since your loved one is not there to share the meal with you? How do you begin to care about your own health when life and death are not at stake anymore? You've gotten used to not caring for yourself. In becoming an expert at reading your loved one's health needs, you lost the read on your own. For the last months you let yourself live with hunger, weight gain (or loss), and exhaustion.

Your old state of health will usually return on its own, but in time. People may want you to make a sudden dramatic healing back to your old physical state of well-being, but do what feels right to you. Remind yourself to eat a bit better or do a little more. But don't give in to everyone's opinion that you have to jump right back in and have a makeover. This is your time to rest and get back in touch with yourself and see how you feel—now.

Go slowly. Do not take on more than you can handle. It's okay to have distractions. Accomplishing those little things in life can take you away from the enormous pain, and some people need a time of doing nothing, while others need to keep busy. Feeling productive can be a welcome change at times.

For those left with little to do after a death, taking care of themselves may feel forced. You may not have the motivation to exercise or even take a walk around the block. You may not care about food. After all, food and exercise didn't help keep your loved one alive.

Some may no longer care about eating anymore, while others may have the opposite reaction and overeat. Food can temporarily seem to help with the emptiness, but just like any temporary feeling of relief, overeating is not a long-term solution in dealing with loss. As you grieve and learn to live with this loss, those unhealthy solutions will usually fade.

Those left behind may have to return to work right away. Work too will feel different. You may be slower at work or not at your peak. You might not take on additional tasks. No one will expect you to go the extra mile at work during this time. Don't try to do things exactly as you used to, because you are different now. Be your own guide. If work feels too much for you, slow down, take the time you need. If your business is a place of busyness that gives your mind and body a break from all that hurts you, use it.

Whether you are the type to eat less or more, exercise less or more, or move one step back from working a lot or diving in, you must take enough time to help your body repair. It's a good idea to go to bed earlier, sleep a little later. If you're out of balance, take little steps. Try to eat a little better, exercise a little, and be good to yourself, and don't be surprised if you get sick more often than usual. Your body's defenses have been weakened and your resistance is lowered. It is not unusual for people to get sick after a loved one has died; a cold or flu may come on suddenly and hang on a little longer than usual.

Daniel had been married for twenty-four years to Rachel, the love of his life. During her slow demise due to heart problems, he was utterly dedicated to her. When she died, he felt lost and went back to work right away. Before the first week was over he began feeling pain in his head that turned into the worst headache he'd ever had.

He went to the emergency room, where they were beginning to order tests for possible internal bleeding or something even worse, perhaps a tumor. He told them he had not hurt his head, and one doctor, after examining his scalp, said, "Cancel the tests. He has shingles." The doctor went on to ask Daniel if he'd been under any unusual stress lately.

"The worst you can imagine," he said.

Before long the shingles, caused by the same virus that causes chicken pox, was all over his body. It seems that the virus lies dormant in the body until severe stress activates it. Daniel had no idea that the pain could stop him in his tracks. There was no rushing back to work or even working from home. He literally had to do nothing while parts of his body became covered with a rash of red patches that blistered. They left behind crusts, which fell off eventually, exposing pink healing skin.

In subsequent appointments with his regular doctor, the physician remarked, "This doesn't surprise me. I often see people get ill with something after a huge loss."

Daniel's body gave him no choice but to stop and grieve, a good demonstration that if you move fast before your body is ready, it will tell you. It's much better to shift all that wonderful attention you had for your loved one back to your own body in a healthy way. It is what they would want, as many dying people worry about the living.

Take the time to take care of yourself. If you become ill, it may be the body's way of saying, "slow down." Maybe you need a weekend at home, a day in bed, or even a day of being pampered.

Take care of *yourself*.

SO MUCH TO DO

There is so much to do: make the calls, make the plans, make the arrangements. To many, this sense of being busy is a blessing; what else could possibly seem worthy of your time? If we sat and felt the emptiness, it would be too much. So most of us dive in and do all that needs to be done. We want it done the way we think is best, the way that would honor our loved one. We need the rituals and all the tasks that go with them. Take comfort in the busyness; it is an integral part of the mourning process.

Some feel rushed, as if they rode the scariest roller coaster of their lives and now there is *more* to do. They feel pushed and hurried through the feelings and tasks. Sometimes the rituals themselves make them feel that way and sometimes it is just the circumstances: the transportation, the accommodations, the guests, the visitors, the meals. Whatever it is, slow down and take your time. There is a richness in such rituals that brings a framework to loss. Try not to rush through this process, since the rituals are designed to help you find meaning and a way to externalize and share your pain. To speed through it would cause you to miss the opportunity.

Judith wanted everything to be exactly right for Frank's funeral. She made the plans, everything was in place, and on the day of the funeral Judith was rushing around double- and triple-checking everything. Was the reception room ready? Was the food coming on time? She even confirmed the caterers four times on her cell phone and all was ready. But when her sister, Eloise, arrived, she saw the state Judith was in. While the rituals can help us, we can also get lost in the planning. Eloise tried to get Judith away from all the completed tasks, but she couldn't get her alone for a second.

"These maps for the guests need your immediate attention," said Eloise in a final attempt to be alone with Judith. She didn't want to discuss maps, she wanted to help Judith understand the uniqueness of this day in the mourning process and help her realize the planning part of the funeral was over.

Eloise grabbed her sister's hand and said, "I know how much you want everything to be just right for Frank. And it will be fine, or if there are some glitches we will make it through. But more importantly, Judith, this is the one and only time that all these people will ever gather together for Frank . . . and for you. You will continue to see about thirty percent of these people, but the majority you will never see again. Today, though, they're here to share their sorrow and yours. Today is the day they will openly and tenderly share their love for Frank, and you will grieve, for the rest of your life, mostly alone. Today, you have the opportunity to grieve with so many others, and I would hate to see you miss that." Judith was then able to stop and be fully present for the funeral and the shared grief.

For many it may seem as if other people are moving too fast. Sometimes it seems as if everything feels rushed because the death seemed to come too soon. You may be trying to get to the next moment too quickly or to handle all the logistics in a rushed style. Or you may feel as if you've got to move through decisions too quickly. You need to do what you feel is right, not what you feel is quick. Rituals can be meaningful to you, and you have to take care of funeral arrangements, but it's okay to say, I need a little time here to catch my breath. I need a moment.

Take time to feel your feelings and to experience them. Let your friends help, and do not turn down offers of support. And take a moment to be real. When someone asks how you are, don't automatically say, "Fine." Instead, you could say, "I'm having a tough time, so thank you for checking on me." Or "I need help but I don't know what to ask for."

Very few of us are used to saying, "I'm okay, but check back with me in a month." Let yourself receive the help, the support, the love. If you want to make a particular call personally or do a particular task yourself, fine. If you don't, allow a friend or family member to help.

When Oliver's wife, Lauren, died, he accepted every invitation from friends and family for dinner after work. If a friend offered golf on Saturday, he said yes. If his sister suggested brunch on Sunday, he was there. He kept busy, there seemed always to be a lot to do, and his friends were happy that Oliver remained active and involved in life. No one questioned it.

But one month later, Oliver started declining all the invites. A friend became concerned and asked Oliver, "Why are you suddenly turning us down? My wife says it's important that you don't isolate. We thought you were doing so well."

Oliver replied, "I needed to keep busy all the time at first, but now I'm feeling strong enough to just stay home and do nothing. It may look like isolation, but it's just time for me to slow down."

When it's time for you to start making plans with friends, do what feels right to you and what you feel your loved one would have wanted. If you need help, ask for guidance from family, friends, neighbors, the hospital staff, the mortuary, your church or synagogue. Listen to what they have to say, then take what works for you and leave the rest. You can't please everybody. Do not let yourself be swayed by anyone or anything that does not feel right to you or does not honor your loved one's memory.

Do the best you can and let that be enough. Be sure to take time alone if you need it, and ask for company if you need that.

Cry whenever and wherever you want.

CLOTHES AND POSSESSIONS

While there is so much going on inside of you, a myriad of tasks await outside. One of these tasks is to pack up your loved one's clothing. Another is to decide what to do with it. This often feels like the most difficult job of all, because to deal with a person's possessions is to clearly face the fact they are gone. If they were still here, we would not be going through their things—it would be an intrusion on their privacy. The bottom line is that glasses, shoes, and coats force our acceptance of a harsh reality.

The emotions of going through someone's things will be enormous, possibly overwhelming. With the smell or the touch of their fabric, clothes remind us of the one we love and the moments we spent together and their likes and dislikes. Their watches, rings, and other pieces of jewelry remind us of their style and personality. Most of all, their clothes and belongings emphasize their absence in our lives.

Start this task when you feel strong enough. Ask a friend or family member to do it with you if you feel that a loving presence will help. If you cannot face going through your loved one's possessions, ask a family member or neighbor for help. Not everyone wants to go through a loved one's clothes, and you may feel as if you have been through enough.

And then, even if you wanted to sort through your loved one's possessions, you may not have the time. Work within your constraints and get help if you are pressured for time. Also feel free to keep a number of things that you may "just not feel sure of yet."

After the death of her mother, a daughter came to town from out of state to pack up her mother's apartment. When it came to the closets, she felt rushed, so she packed a couple of suitcases with her mother's clothes. "It was too soon to give her clothes away," she said, taking them back home with her. At a later date, when she was less emotional and rushed, she sorted through the clothing at her leisure. She discovered that the task before her was much more than organizing and redistributing personal belongings. It was more than going through a home, its contents, its closets, and its drawers. It was the physical and personal reminders of someone she deeply cared for and cherished. She was glad she could spend time with her mother's things, perfect reminders of who her mother was in life.

Loved ones are often highly insulted when a friend or family member says, "Can I have their bicycle or cookbook, I need one," not recognizing they are not asking for an item. The thing they now consider a leftover object was an important part of our loved one. The truth is that each physical possession has a story, a memory—some of them known, others unknown. Here is his favorite suit, which he wore a lot. Here is the chair she loved to sit in and watch TV. The nightstand by the bed even tells a story; how it went suddenly from the clutter of remotes and novels to medical necessities. Even going through the music they listened to can become a vivid personal glimpse into a loved one's life, an emotional landscape that we may dread and want to put off. Or we may want to look forward to the reminiscing that comes with it. The process, usually some combination of the two, is as varied and personal as who we are and who our loved one was.

Betty was a loving grandma with big brown eyes and a smile that made you wish she were your grandmother. She never went to visit anyone's home empty-handed, and when you visited her, you would also get a gift: nothing big, just something lying around that she thought was perfect for you. Betty had her rituals, like never giving away things to charity without washing and ironing them. If a pair of pants was missing a button, she would put one on. And she never gave away a wallet or purse without putting a penny in it for good luck.

Her son, Greg, and daughter-in-law, Nicole, joked that she had made many people rich by giving them a penny. Betty had become more of a mother to Nicole after Nicole's mom died five years prior, telling her that whenever she found a penny someone in heaven was thinking of her. If you asked her about it, she was likely to start singing "Pennies from Heaven." But if she was with Nicole and found a penny, she would say, "This is from your mom. She is thinking about you and watching over you like a good mother."

After Betty died, Greg and Nicole had the job of going through her apartment and giving things away to charity, no small job since they felt the need to clean everything and make it look as good as possible before giving it away. Greg found it enormously difficult to go through his mother's belongings and decide what things to keep and what to give away. In her closet, he found a crocodile purse that Nicole had given Betty for her birthday. He remembered how cute Nicole thought the purse was and how Betty loved it. Greg thought he would put it aside to give back to Nicole.

After they had finished taking care of Betty's belongings, Greg meticulously cleaned the crocodile purse. He turned the bag upside down and wiped the inside out thoroughly. When he was finished the bag looked like new. He then put the finishing touch on it with a penny in the small spare key compartment before he put it in a box with wrapping paper and a bow.

He hid it for Nicole's next birthday. When the evening came a few months later, Greg gave Nicole a beautiful necklace for her birthday. After dinner Nicole became teary-eyed talking about how much she missed her mom. Then she said, "I bet our moms are in heaven right now thinking about us too."

Greg suddenly remembered the purse. "Hang on," he said, "I have one more gift for you." He handed her the box and added, "Mom would have wanted you to have this."

Nicole was delighted when she saw the purse, immediately noticing that Greg had put two pennies in the small spare key compartment. Greg turned white. "I only put in one penny," he said. "You have no idea how I cleaned that purse and checked every inch. I can tell you without a doubt that there was no penny there until I put one in."

Nicole took Greg's hand and said, "Your mother always told me that my mom was thinking of me in heaven whenever she found a penny. I guess she still wanted me to know that our moms are together again watching over us."

The ritual of dealing with a loved one's clothes and belongings facilitates the grieving process, partly by helping us accept the reality of the loss. The simple act of giving clothes away to someone who otherwise could not afford them is one of the many ways that your loved one continues to have a positive impact on the world. A dining room set and special china can be a connection of one generation to another. Keeping your mother's favorite scarf, or a tie that your husband loved, is an additional keepsake that will remind you of a special feeling you had with them and for them, always.

HOLIDAYS

"Holidays are time spent with loved ones" was imprinted on our psyche from a young age. Every family has its own traditions and unique ways of celebrating holidays. When we grow up, we usually update them and make them our own, but original imprints of how holidays are spent usually transcend generations.

Holidays mark the passage of time in our lives. They are part of the milestones we share with each other, and they generally represent time spent with family. They bring meaning to certain days and we bring much meaning back to them. But since holidays are for being with those we love the most, how on earth can anyone be expected to cope with them when a loved one has died? For many people, this is the hardest part of grieving, when we miss our loved ones even more than usual.

How can you celebrate togetherness when there is none? When you have lost someone special, your world loses its celebratory qualities. Holidays only magnify the loss. The sadness feels sadder and the loneliness goes deeper. The need for support may be the greatest during the holidays.

Nevertheless, for some, it makes sense to just ignore the holidays as if they didn't exist. The alternative of just going through the motions without any meaning might seem pointless—the worst loneliness of all—so why not just cancel them for a year?

Berry Perkins knew she had to allow her teenage boys the space to grieve when her husband, actor Anthony Perkins, died. After his death, Berry and her sons, like so many other families, tried to carry on. Luckily Berry was very intuitive and knew when something was not working and that grief needed its space. She said, "Holidays were so important to us as a family, and suddenly there was this huge void. Every holiday is a bombardment, a hole that reminds us that he is not here. We tried to recreate these holidays and we thought we could carry on doing things the way we had always done. But we learned quickly we couldn't do it the way we had always done it before, not without Tony. It was just too hard and sad.

"The first Christmas, we kind of glided through, because we thought, 'Okay, we are going to do this.' The second Christmas, we put up the tree but it took us a week to hang the decorations. We needed time to grieve without trying to have a happy time. We were all so sad. Then we came to a mutual agreement to take a break from Christmas for a couple of years. We decided when we came back to Christmas again, we would start a new tradition."

Berry knew to not keep up the pretense of happy holidays when she and her children were grieving. She knew what was right for them, and she taught her children to honor their feelings. After a break and some healing time, Berry and her family were able to celebrate the holidays again, not the way they had before, but in new ways.

Berry Perkins was a wise woman, and it was a terrible twist of fate that she died in one of the hijacked airplanes on 9/11. Hopefully the grief lessons she gave to her sons helped them through their second tragedy.

For others in grief, staying involved with the holidays is a symbol of life continuing. For them, celebrating the holidays creates a time to be with other loved ones and not to feel so alone. It is a time for some to find meaning and to reflect upon all that has been lost.

Many find it difficult *not* to observe the holiday but don't want to pretend. You can integrate the loss into the holiday by giving it a time and a place. Perhaps the prayer before dinner includes your loved one. Maybe you light a candle for her. A simple gesture of recognizing your loved one can reflect the continued presence in your heart. Some elect to leave the festivities early, to have some time alone with their loss. Making time for your loss and acknowledging it is often easier than resisting it.

Sometimes our loved one's death is linked to a certain holiday. We remember they died before Valentine's Day, or on Mother's or Father's day. We never forget they died right after Easter, or that was their last Passover. Maybe they died near the Fourth of July. From then on, the holidays will never be the same. Since the holidays are markers, even if your loved one didn't die near one, you still look back and think, that was their last Thanksgiving or last Christmas. Some knew it would be their last holiday and some didn't. Either way a formerly joyous holiday becomes a time of sorrow.

Sixteen-year-old Amy went into her mother's room on New Year's Eve. Her mother had been dealing with kidney disease for many years, and Amy wished her a Happy New Year. Then Amy whispered in her ear, "This will be the year you get a transplant." The mother died four days later. Had she lived, Amy might or might not have thought of her mother every New Year's; but in that moment her death and that holiday became forever linked.

The holidays are a time to review your traditions and decide what you want to do. For some, the changes they experience during the holidays are temporary, whereas for others, they're permanent. Marie always sent out cards with a picture of her husband and herself from their most recent vacation. After he died she did not want to carry on that tradition. In fact, when she examined it more closely she realized it was not a part of the holiday she enjoyed. It had begun as a fun thing to do years ago, but in truth it had lost its fun way before her husband died. For Marie, grief provided the opportunity to release traditions that may have lost their meaning anyway.

For others it can be a time of complete reorganization. Joyce, a teacher in her early fifties, said that after she lost her husband, she started out by lying low during the holidays. "I decided," she said, "that grief gave me the permission to really evaluate what parts of the holidays I enjoyed and what parts I didn't. If I was going to rebuild the holidays, I knew the old way was not an option. Probably for the first time, I took the time to make them personal."

There is no right or wrong way to handle the holidays in grief. You have to decide what is right for you and do it. You have every right to change your mind, even a few times. Friends and family members may not have a clue how to help you through the holidays, and you may not either. If you do know, give the people around you clear messages. For instance, you can tell them, "This year I don't want the responsibility of cooking the family dinner." Or you may find it important that you continue to do that. Just let people know. Tell them you want to talk about your loved one, or let them know you are just too raw and don't want to. Don't be afraid to change things to suit your needs. People feel very pulled to do things they often don't want to do during the holidays, and this is your chance to make your needs known.

Many people have had too much change and need the familiarity of the seasons. Bill felt that his wife had enough Christmas spirit for both of them, but after she died, there was not enough Christmas spirit left for one. He felt that any attempt would only make him feel worse, so he used the holiday to travel to Alaska. "I needed a change of environment," he said. "I'd always wanted to see Alaska and I felt like I could manage exploring a new place, while I could not have managed Christmas and New Year's without my wife at home."

It is very natural to feel you may *never* enjoy the holidays again. They will certainly never be the same as they were. However, in time, most people are able to find meaning again in the traditions as a new form of the holiday spirit grows inside of them.

When death occurs before it, a holiday can remain unfinished. Gina's mother had the family's gifts under the Christmas tree when the call came to Gina on December 22: her mother had suffered a massive stroke, and she died two weeks later. The Christmas tree and presents sat untouched by the family, like a deserted town.

After New Year's, the family solemnly opened up their gifts for each other, but no one knew what to do about her mother's gifts, so they just sat there. During January, Gina helped her father pack up her mother's belongings and put her remaining affairs in order, but she would not allow the tree or gifts to be touched. "Christmas was frozen in time for me," she said. "Opening the gifts would be too hard and I had no idea what to do with my gifts to my mother."

She took down the tree at the end of January and left the presents in the corner. She and her father agreed that they were starting to look like an unmarked grave and felt that way, too. Her dad helped her pack up the boxes and put them in a closet. The following Christmas, when Gina was out of shock and ready to receive the gifts from her mother, one by one she opened them and felt her mother's presence as well as her presents. Her father opened the gifts that were intended for his wife and commented on how she would have loved them.

Even if you decide not to do the holidays after a loved one's death, they are hard to ignore. Everyone around may wish you happy holidays without any idea that you are grieving, since the holidays continue despite your deep sadness. You continue on with your loved one's loud absence.

We are often acutely aware of the Thanksgiving, Christmas, and Hanukkah season, but we forget how hard Mother's Day might be without a mother or how empty Father's Day may feel without a father. You will never have another mother or father again, and you may feel completely left out of this holiday, unlike the others. People find ways to remember their mothers and fathers and honor them long after they are gone. Some honor them by becoming mothers and fathers. Some do it with a simple, kind thought of love. That is the uniqueness of the loss of a parent.

Rob and Cindy were unable to celebrate the holidays after their seventeen-year-old son died. They understood that for the next few years, the holidays would be unfixable, so they decided to spend the time serving others. On Thanksgiving they went to the local homeless shelter and served dinner. On Christmas they helped wrap presents for local foster homes. In the end, their action served more than they had expected, because it took their mind off the intensity of their loss and helped them see that they were not alone in their pain and misfortune.

Holidays are clearly some of the roughest terrain we navigate after a loss. The ways we handle them are as individual as we are. What is vitally important is that we be present for the loss in whatever form the holidays do or don't take. These holidays are part of the journey to be felt fully. They are usually very sad, but sometimes we may catch ourselves doing okay, and we may even have a brief moment of laughter. Whatever you experience, just remember that sadness is *allowed*, because death, as they say, doesn't take a holiday.

Even without grief, our friends and relatives often think they know how our holidays should look, what "the family" should and shouldn't do.

Now more than ever, be gentle with yourself and protect yourself.

Don't do more than you want, and don't do anything that does not serve your soul and your loss.

LETTER WRITING

Grief must be externalized. Our pain and sadness can be fully realized only when we release them. For many, writing letters to their loved one is a convenient, always available way to get the words out and communicate. What—or even why—should you write to someone with whom communication seems to be lost?

As far back as we can remember, writing has been a tool to help us say, "We were here." In a historical sense, to say who we were and what happened to us matters. Ancient writings may have been created to communicate with others in the area and perhaps even to communicate with future generations. But they always originated with a longing to connect. That longing is never stronger than when a deep connection has been broken.

Amelia found whenever she most missed her sister, Lydia, she would stop what she was doing and write to her. Sometimes it was just a note with one sentence on it and other times it was five pages. She unknowingly went through many of the five stages in her letters over time. Her early letters were about her denial, how tough it was to believe that Lydia was gone, how she kept feeling that Lydia must be away on a long vacation.

She then wrote diatribes about what life was like without her and how angry she was that Lydia had left her alone in the world. She wrote of feeling depressed about how they would not go through old age together, of wondering about all the "what ifs" in her sister's medical care. Finally, though, she reached a point of acknowledging that Lydia was truly gone and was not coming back. Then she wrote that although she was finally accepting her sister's death, she didn't like the acceptance one little bit.

For Amelia, the letter writing was not only a form of externalizing her loss. It was also the form that her grief took, an outlet that worked best for her as it facilitated her working through the stages. She just did it on paper. Years later it was easy for her to see her grief and healing in her words. It also gave permanent witness to all that she had felt and lost. It was the record of her pain and healing.

Writing is a wonderful companion to our loneliness in a world where we stand alone. Many people write about their feelings after a loss. Some write in a grief journal to deposit their feelings without worrying about someone else's reactions. In any case writing externalizes what is in us. Those circulatory thoughts can find an exit with the pen and paper or with the keyboard and mouse. For many, writing feels better than speaking, as the unspoken healing can come through journaling. You can find your voice in writing in a way that you can't find in other forms of communication. You can also finish your unfinished business in letter writing.

We are filled with so many memories, feelings, hopes, dreams, stories, insights, reactions, and questions that are all wanting to get out and take their rightful place. The written word can be their expression.

The written word can also be a communication to our loved one, as we are often left with things unsaid. We believe that death is not the end of communication, and if you have something to say in your heart, your loved ones will feel it in theirs.

Write to them even after they are gone. Tell them how you are doing and how much you miss them. A letter can be a substitute trip to a distant grave when frequent travel is not possible. Write what you would say if you were there. You may find you have a collection of letters and may want to read them when you are next able to visit your loved one's grave. You may find the letters were just for you.

You may find comfort in reading old letters and cards that the two of you gave to each other. Letters have a special power in that they are tangible evidence that our loved one took the time and effort to sit and write on the very paper we hold in front of us. Letters comfort us and often outlive us. The proof of someone's presence exists in his or her handwriting.

We write to express ourselves, but sometimes we can write to ask for an answer. How on earth can you receive an answer from a loved one who has died? One technique that we have found to produce interesting results is to write the letter to your loved one with your dominant hand. Now get a fresh sheet of paper and allow yourself to write a letter back from your loved one with your nondominant hand. For example, if you are right-handed, your nondominant hand will be your left.

Miriam missed her mother terribly since her death. Miriam was a strategic planner for a large educational firm and missed her Sunday get-togethers with her mother, the grounding she had come to count upon on a weekly basis. Miriam decided she'd write her mom a letter. She would write the letter as she normally would, with her right hand, and then write a reply from her mother, using her left hand to receive the answer from her mom.

In her first letter, Miriam wrote about how much she missed talking to her, how busy she was at work, and how well things were going. But she still felt a terrible void. Then she added that she was relieved that her mother was no longer sick or in pain.

She was a bit skeptical about the process but felt she had written her letter with sincerity and had nothing to lose. When she switched to her nondominant hand and began to write back, she was surprised how the letter seemed to flow. Her mother reassured her that she was okay and missed her too. Then she went on to say, "I miss our Sundays too, and I loved our discussions, but I also had another reason for them. You were never a good eater, and that way I made sure you got one good meal a week. You haven't been eating well lately."

Miriam was startled by the response and believed it was her mother writing back to her. Her mother was always the cook and the mother, making sure Miriam ate right, and now she felt a bit less alone in the world, feeling that somehow her mother was still there. She would continue to do this handwriting exercise whenever she was really missing her mother.

This form of letter writing has been comforting to many people, even when we're not sure of what is happening. Neil and his wife, Michelle, were in deep grief after the loss of their boy, Max, who had just turned eight. Michelle decided to use the letter-writing process to talk to Max. She cried as she wrote how sorry she was that he would not have a full life and would never get to have a million normal experiences.

In his letter back, Max told her that even though it was hard to understand, it was his time. He reassured her she would see him again and that he was okay. He told her that it would take her many years to understand this loss and that they would have "more kids," and he wanted it that way. He mentioned several times that she would have more kids.

After she received the letter, Michelle didn't get the sense of comfort she'd hoped for. She loved knowing that he was okay but felt it was too soon to even be thinking about another child, much less several. A few days later she missed a menstrual period. She got a home pregnancy test and was shocked to see she was pregnant.

She didn't know how to deal with the possibility of being pregnant so soon after the loss of her son, and she made an appointment to see her doctor. In the next couple of days she and her husband talked of nothing else, and both agreed that a new baby coming so soon after Max's death was poor timing. Michelle put the letter-writing out of her mind—until the doctor announced she was pregnant with twins.

"It's okay," she said, suddenly smiling. "I know it's okay."

Her husband did not understand her peacefulness until they were home and she showed him the letter she wrote from Max, as he went on and on about them having "more kids."

It can be argued that Michelle unconsciously knew she was pregnant with twins and that she, rather than her dead son, had produced the letter.

The point is that she derived *comfort* from the letter writing. In the end, that's all that matters.

FINANCES

People generally don't want to talk openly about their finances, but as these play a role in life, they also play a role in grief. We know we can't take it with us when we die, but when a loved one dies, money can be a complicated matter. The complications involve having either too little or too much and depend on how well you are prepared to deal with your finances after a death. We can make matters worse with all of our emotions around finances, but the truth is that money is a tool. It is in itself neutral, neither good nor bad. It is what we do with our money and how we perceive it that decides whether we feel good or bad about it.

Allan and Paige never really made a decent living. A house-painter who dreamed of being an artist, Allan had met Paige in his twenties when he signed up for a community college class she taught on the great Italian masters. They fell in love and were soon married, but while many of their friends were taking inexpensive Las Vegas honeymoons, they dreamed of going to the art galleries in Florence, Italy. But they would have to save up the money.

They were in their early twenties when they had one child, then a second and a third. Kids, house payments, and day-to-day expenses soon got in the way, and Allan got busy painting houses. A far cry from Italy, but they kept their dream alive.

By the time they were in their forties, the kids were teenagers and they had saved enough money to put them through college. That would leave half the money they needed for their long-awaited honeymoon. But soon their dreams were shattered: Allan's friend drove up to Paige's house one day and suggested she sit down. Allan had fallen off a scaffold and plunged three stories, breaking his neck, dying instantly.

Paige was devastated by all that she had lost. But when Allan's boss informed her that she would be the recipient of the company's life insurance policy, now doubled since Allan's death was accidental, Paige was instantly wealthy. Now she realized the sad irony that she could take off to Florence any time she wanted, but she would have to do it alone.

Paige had to mourn all they had wanted to do together, all the dreams that would never be fulfilled. And there was another complication. Every time she spent any of the money on anything, she felt enormously guilty. To exchange a life of thrift for one of financial independence had been possible only through Allan's death, a tragic irony.

Most of us dream about having more money, but we have mixed emotions when the money is tied to death. We may feel good that our loved one cared for us and protected us, but it sometimes feels like tainted money, tough to enjoy when its origin is loss.

Many people have to find a way to make peace with this situation. Some do it by never spending the money. Others do it by spending it as quickly as possible. Still others spend it in a way that does some good in the world, understanding that although the sudden financial boon feels good, it is not a trade-off for loss. And then, many are not prepared to manage it, no matter if it is a fortune or enough for their day-to-day bills.

Lamar always handled the finances in the family. After he died, his wife, Hanna, had no idea how to write a check. In her grief, she did not want to learn about deposits, checks, automatic bill payments. She said, "Nothing is really automatic if I don't know what I am doing. The last time I dealt with money, I put a paycheck in the bank and wrote out a check for rent and lights. Now I've got a notice 'the automatic debit was not honored and the money had been reversed.' I had no idea what any of it meant."

Hanna's story is common when one person in the family takes responsibility for the finances. No matter how hard or simple the money matters are, if you are not used to doing it, it is just one more thing that makes loss harder to take and grief longer to heal. Even if they had been doing the finances all along, many have shared how they had a tougher time after they suffered a loss, since they felt more alone in their financial world. In the past, if anything went wrong moneywise, at least they were not alone. Now they have no partner and it's completely up to them.

Meg and her husband, Dale, were determined to beat his cancer. Despite the prognosis from the community hospital, they decided to go to a well-known cancer clinic in New York, where Dale spent two months in expensive treatments. When their money ran out, they traveled to Mexico for alternative treatments, refusing to give up. They even cashed in Dale's life insurance policy, hoping and praying to save his life, but it didn't work.

When Dale died, Meg was so broke, she had to borrow money for the funeral and file for bankruptcy. Her grief was compounded by her new world, which did not include her husband or any resources, for that matter. But she took comfort in the knowledge that she had done everything possible for her husband.

Death can give focus to what money can and cannot buy. It can teach us what being rich is all about. We learn that no amount of money can ever replace the loss of someone we love.

Suzette knew from the day she married Jason that his parents did not like her. They had hoped their son, a stockbroker, would marry a financial equal, but Suzette, a teacher, did not come from money. During the next twenty-two years, the family were cordial and even nice at times, which led Suzette to believe that they had finally accepted her.

When Jason had a stroke, she left her teaching career to care for him for the next two years until he died. After the funeral, she went back to her hometown for a week to be with her family, but when she returned, she discovered that most of the furnishings in her house had been removed, even the curtains. She was calling the police when her mother-in-law showed up with a trust deed in hand.

"Most of these pieces were family heirlooms," she said, "but you can have the 'other stuff.' "

"What other stuff?" asked Suzette. "You took the bed we slept in every night of our lives together."

"Well," said the mother-in-law brusquely, "it's a very important antique that belongs in the family."

Suzette had thought she was family by then. Now, not only had she lost her husband, she also felt betrayed by those she had long considered family. She realized their opinion of her had never changed after all those years. She spent the next few years fighting over the trust. Unfortunately we have heard many such stories about how the funeral arrangements have barely been made when someone swoops in and makes sure the will gets read and the finances distributed.

Grief is a time when we try to find our wholeness again after all has been lost. But finances can often create a distraction from the grieving process. It's better to let those financial disagreements go and just focus on healing. We understand this is not very practical and it is hard to let go of finances, since they often symbolize family, union, togetherness, and a piece of all that has been ripped apart. In many cases, since money means survival, it's hard to grieve when you're not sure you can pay the rent. But grief is a sad, soft spot we must fall into for our healing to begin. If you are in a defensive mode because of money, no matter what the circumstances, it is hard to find that soft spot.

Wealth and poverty are states of mind. Many people without money feel wealthy, while many rich people can feel poor. Death is a factor that changes all our views as we are forced to evaluate our worth and what ultimately matters in life.

AGE

Length of life is one of the ways we measure our time on earth. If your loved one died young, you may feel that the death was premature, that their life was unlived. If your loved one died in midlife, you see someone who did not reach her prime or someone who left without the retirement he was promised. An older person may have had a long life, but it still feels as if it wasn't long enough. For some, many years provided a full life, they may have lived to ninety-eight, but they didn't have quality of life for the last few years. There is every conceivable feeling in between for every possible age at death.

In the early 1980s, in a cystic fibrosis unit of a children's hospital, the average life span was sixteen years if you were lucky. It was easy to look at these kids and say, "How sad they're missing out on sixty years of life." But for the patients, this had always been the reality. They grew up with this truth; they led full lives and some married at twelve, which makes sense if you know you'll most likely be dead at sixteen. They were raised with the harsh reality that they needed only two ingredients for a complete life: birth and death. They did their best to have as complete a life as possible in the years they were given.

The rest of us, on the other hand, require many other necessary ingredients for a full life: college, work, marriage, home, cars, vacations, grandkids, retirement, and old age. To think of having anything less seems a tragedy for most of us. And no matter how much time someone had, no matter how full the life was, it is still a deep loss for us.

For you as the one left behind, your age is also a factor. There is no denying that for the most part, the longer we've lived, the more experiences with loss we have had. Of course there are many exceptions, but more years in the world also provides us with deeper experiences of support systems, problem solving, and emotional maturity, things we didn't have in place when we were younger.

A younger person grieves differently from an elderly one, for many reasons. They have more life in front of them, they have to get back to school, back to work, and maybe back to their own children. Younger people have to get back out into the world, because they still have lives to build and experiences to have.

Becky was devastated when her sister died in college. She felt as if her world had collapsed, but she carried on, never forgetting when her sister would have graduated and what she might have become.

Becky finished school, started her career, got married, and had kids of her own. When her daughter started college and turned twenty-one, Becky saw things differently. "I suddenly realized how young my sister was," she said, "and how huge her death was. I see it so differently with a daughter the same age. I grieved at that time, but I didn't get it fully. I just didn't realize that for the rest of my life, I would never have a sister again. She would never do all the things I would go on to do. There would be no career for her, no marriage, and no kids.

"How could I know that when I was in my twenties? Death was a tragic event, but I had no idea I had only touched the surface of my grief. I only saw what I lost at the time. I didn't understand what she lost. Now that I am in my fifties, I realize how young she was when she died, it being almost thirty years ago now."

An older person in retirement may have more time to think about the loss. They may feel less need to rejoin the world, thinking that they have already seen and done enough. They may have fewer years in front of them and less desire to fill those years with new experiences. This may lead to depression in many cases, while in others it can result in more contentment with what is left.

How we deal with our grief also reflects how our loved one dealt with death. When Blair was dying at seventy-nine years old, her daughter asked, "Mom, are you afraid?"

"Years ago," she told her daughter, "I might have been afraid, but now, I know so many more people who have died than I do people alive. Most of my friends are now dead. I figure if death is nothingness, I won't be dealing with anything. But if there is an afterlife I'll see all the people I love and miss. Wherever I will be, I'm sure I won't be alone, and in time, I know I'll see you again."

As sad as she was, Blair helped her daughter to feel comforted in her grief. She was able to picture her mother seeing her own parents again as well as so many other family members and friends. When we are older, we may fear death less. Sometimes, the absence of fear mixed with the hopes of reuniting with loved ones who have passed connects to those in grief on some level and provides comfort.

When someone dies in their twenties or thirties, we grieve not only for the person but for the years unlived, for all that might have been but wasn't. We feel cheated. But when an older person dies after living a full life, we are generally more comfortable with their passing. Their advanced age makes us feel that they lived a natural life span and things are more in order. For example, President Ronald Reagan's death felt very different from President John Kennedy's death, because of their ages at the time of death and the latter's being assassinated. If John Kennedy had died at age eighty-seven of an illness rather than a gunshot, we may have felt the loss but not the accompanying suffering over a life being cut short.

Old age in many ways cushions us in grief, prepares us, and helps us deal with loss. Young age complicates our grieving by increasing our sense of unfairness. We all believe we should die old, not young. This is why we see a different face of grief as we ourselves age.

CLOSURE

Dictionaries describe *closure* as the "act of closing or the state of being closed; a bringing to an end, a conclusion." In Gestalt psychology it is the "tendency to create ordered and satisfying wholes."

If you look back at the origins of the word, *closure* comes from an old Latin source meaning "closing the gap between two things"—or to enclose so as not to disturb your neighbors. But in modern society, where grief disturbs our neighbors who want to fix and heal us so they don't have to feel their own grief, closure has taken on the clichéd meaning of "wrapping up a situation." We are pressured to find closure on the work situation, the romantic relationship, and even on a death. But how do we find an ending on a process that encompasses the integration and healing not only of a loss but of a person whom we deeply loved?

When we speak about grief, there are two closures that come to mind. The first is the unrealistic wrap-up we expect after a loss. It has become an added burden not just to mourn and grieve the loss, but to find that closure and find it quick so you can move on.

The second kind of closure involves doing things that help put the loss in perspective, such as reviewing what happened and why—or looking for missing pieces of the stories and filling in the gaps. It can range from finding the killer of a loved one to finding a way to say good-bye after a loved one died at the end of a long struggle with illness.

John's birthdays were always big celebrations, mainly because his mother's two best friends' children also had July birthdays. Every year there was a joint party for all, and they loved the idea of doing it all at once. In a year or so, their parents knew that each kid would want a separate celebration, but for now it worked for everyone.

One particular July when it was exceptionally hot, they decided on a pool party. The pool was wall-to-wall kids, who were splashing, cavorting, screaming, and playing. Five-year-old birthday boy Johnny put his left foot in the water, descended the steps into the pool, silently walked in, and kept walking until he was completely underwater. In a few minutes, when his mother, Gwen, saw that he was gone, she frantically cleared everyone out of the water. There was Johnny, on the bottom of the pool, not breathing. The paramedics could not revive him, and his mother kept muttering and repeating, "I was right there. I never heard a thing. He didn't call for help or anything." The paramedics explained that as adults we scream when we drown, but kids often just drown silently and go under without even knowing how to fight.

For the next three years, Gwen talked with everyone who had been at the party, all of whom reassured her that she had been a good mother, that it had happened in a second. By the fifth year, she was still talking about it, and her friends felt it was time to find "closure."

Gwen, however, was baffled by the notion. "How do I find closure for such a tragedy? Every morning I wake up and think,

'Today my child would be ten and in the fourth grade.' How do I find an action that will put this to rest? How long am I allowed for a child that I loved for five years? Can I get an extension because it was an accident?"

In the loss of a young loved one such as Johnny, people may oversimplify the stages. We expect six months of denial, then a few months of anger and depression, followed by some bargaining. Finally we expect to find acceptance, which we imagine will lead to some type of "closure." It's never as easy as items on a checklist. Real life and real grief are never as neat and tidy as that. Many believe that after the death of a child, there is no closure.

Gwen will never find a defining act that will place Johnny in her past. He will never be behind her as if he moved out of the house. He will always be a part of her past and will live in her heart, which makes the concept of closure unrealistic. Gwen survived, and she and her husband had other children, but she never closed the door on Johnny. Instead, she learned to live with a permanent hollowness in her heart. She realized that the only acceptance she could find was that death had happened and that she would develop ways to live with it. But for Gwen, "closure" will never come.

When we approach closure as the actions we take to put loss in perspective, it can be a big help with filling in the gaps. Mary was shocked to get a call that her fifty-year-old husband had suddenly died of a heart attack. She consented to an autopsy, and after a few months, she decided to study the autopsy report. She pored over every detail, looking up every word and medical term she did not understand. Her friends couldn't comprehend why she was being what they called "macabre."

"Understanding what happened," she said, "helps me fill in the gaps; those empty spaces of 'how and why' have some answers now. Nothing will bring him back, but now I have a sense of finality about what happened to his circulatory system. Now I can begin to deal with my own heart."

It is not uncommon for people to order autopsy reports to find out exactly what happened. If they lost a loved one to murder, there often is no rest until the killer is found. Even then, there is often no closure.

Some people, though, find a way to turn their grief into something meaningful for others. When Candy Lightner lost her child to a drunk driving accident, she used her rage to help found the organization MADD, Mothers Against Drunk Driving. John Walsh, of the TV show *America's Most Wanted,* used his grief after the murder of his young son to help find other missing children.

No matter how you work at feeling your feelings fully, you never really find the closure that you hear about or see in movies. But you do find a place for loss, a way to hold it and live with it.

We have often spoken about unfinished business with the dying as they try to die knowing they did the best they could, but no one gets to finish everything. The dying ultimately must accept that their lives are now complete just as they are. In grieving we mistakenly think we can finish everything, but grief is not a project with a beginning and an end. It is a reflection of a loss that never goes away. We simply learn to live with it, both in the foreground and in the background. Where grief fits in our lives is an individual *thing*, often based on how far we have come in integrating the loss.

We have never asked anyone, "Have you found closure?" and found that they responded with a solid yes. The concept refers to bringing some *thing* to a close, like a misunderstanding, a project, or a school year.

You don't ever bring the grief over a loved one to a close.

4. Specific Circumstances

CHILDREN

A grief counselor shared the story of seven-year-old Janis, who asked her father why her mother hadn't gotten out of bed for a month. Her dad, a great believer in telling the truth, said, "She's tired because she's dying of cancer." Janis began to cry and walked out of the room.

For the next two weeks, she sobbed and comforted her mom by saying over and over, "I'm so sorry you're dying." Her mom was too weak to respond, and she died without being able to talk to her daughter.

For the next several years, Janis remained a sad little girl. Whenever someone asked her why she was so unhappy she said, "My mother died." That was reason enough for most people, including her father, who believed that in time, she would come out of her pain naturally.

Janis was in her junior year of high school when her astronomy class was studying the constellations. When they got to the stars that make up the constellation Cancer, Janis's eyes began to tear up. The teacher took note but waited till the bell rang to talk to her. He asked her why she was crying. "Did a boyfriend break up with you?"

"No," she said. "My astrological sign is Cancer. My mom died of me."

Of course the teacher and her father had discussions with Janis to help her understand that she was not the cause of her mother's death. She eventually understood, but for eight years she had lived under the burden of irrational guilt.

Parents often make the mistake of telling their children nothing when it comes to death. Even though Janis's father had the best intentions when he told her about her mother's cancer, like many children, she added her own interpretation. The trouble is that sometimes a child's interpretation is so illogical, we adults never even think of it as a possibility.

Children do not have the resources or experience to integrate loss into their world. In their minds they often fill in gaps with thoughts like, "It must somehow be *my* fault." Unfortunately the person who should be shepherding them through their grief is the surviving parent, who is often too lost in his or her own grief. It would never have occurred to Janis's father to include a discussion of how the astrological sign Cancer is different from her mom's illness. This is why it is not one talk we should have with children, but a series of discussions.

Children are old enough to grieve if they are old enough to love; they are the "forgotten grievers." The surviving parent is often so overwhelmed with emotions that he or she is doing everything possible just to get through a day. It isn't unusual for the most caring parent in the world to forget a child's birthday because of grief, and children don't know how to make their needs known or to articulate loss. They often lack the words to put to their emotions, and since their lives are just beginning, how can we expect them to understand life's endings?

Children simply need to be told ahead of time that they will feel mixed emotions. We say it is jointly the responsibility of the parents, the schools, and the religious communities to teach them about life. But everyone always assumes someone else will deal with a child's grief. In reality it's everyone's responsibility to talk about grief with kids. They know that adults are dealing with major feelings. And so the adults must model grief for the children who take emotional cues from them.

They may not understand all that they see adults going through, but even a limited understanding is important. How children experience early loss will be replayed at many different junctions of their lives. It may determine how safe the world feels, what their friendships are like, and how their romantic relationships play out.

Jesse was six years old when his mother came home and told him that his favorite uncle, who had lived with them, had died of a brain tumor. He climbed into his mother's lap and cried. But in the midst of his weeping his mother got up, walked away, went into her room, and shut the door behind her. His uncle was never mentioned again, and Jesse was neither invited to the funeral nor told about it.

One afternoon he went into the room where his uncle had lived and looked around. The room appeared empty, and his uncle's absence was intensely felt as Jesse looked for some sign that he had existed. Then he spotted his uncle's brown suitcase with fishing stickers on it, at the back of the closet. He remembered helping his uncle put some of those stickers on, the uncle's larger hand pressing gently over his own to make sure the stickers were applied perfectly.

Jesse carried the suitcase into his own room. No one ever missed it or asked about it. He kept that suitcase throughout his childhood and into adulthood. Now he looks back and realizes that it represented a connection to his uncle, especially at a time when he had nothing from his parents but empty space and silence. In essence, that suitcase, a transitional object that held old memories, gave focus to his loss and helped him grieve. It helped him remember the places and things that he and his uncle had seen and done together and gave him a tangible connection. Though Jesse was left without a ritual for his loss, he created his own. Many children, however, do not do as well as Jesse did. Often, the ideas they make up to explain the unexplained are worse than the truth.

Rachel was celebrating Hanukkah with her son, Steven, for the first time since her husband died. When they lit the first candle, she wondered if she should talk about her husband's absence. But when she saw Steven happily opening his first night's gift, she didn't want to ruin his fun or make her son sad, and so she said nothing.

The second and third nights of Hanukkah were the same. When she asked a few friends if she should talk about Steven's dad, they thought he had experienced enough sadness. On the fourth night of Hanukkah, Rachel still felt awkward about not mentioning her son's father, who had been with them for Steven's entire ten years. At bedtime that night she said, "Honey, I don't want to upset you, but it feels strange not mentioning your dad. I don't want to ruin your Hanukkah."

He looked right into her fearful eyes. "Mom," he said, "I've thought about Dad every single night, but I didn't want to say anything to upset *you* either." They spent the next hour laughing and crying about their previous nights of Hanukkah, and they both felt much better after grieving together.

Jesse's and Steven's stories are not unusual. We often imagine that our children don't think about deceased loved ones on birthdays, holidays, and other significant days. But they do, even if they appear to be fine. We just don't realize that if the adult says nothing, that's a message to a kid that we don't hurt anymore or that speaking of the deceased loved one is taboo. When we do talk about it, we send the message that it's okay to remember, to reminisce, and to grieve.

A grief counselor remembered the story of a teacher, John Morrison. Known to his sixth-grade students as Mr. Morrison, he was close with one of his students, Greg, with whom he shared a love of science. When Greg's mother died, Mr. Morrison thought he would wait for Greg to say something. Days turned to weeks, weeks to months, and before they knew it the year was up and it was time for Greg to go to middle school. Mr. Morrison remembered his favorite student well and felt sad for his loss of his mother. He believed he had respected Greg's privacy in not talking about it.

When Greg was seventeen he ran into Mr. Morrison in a store where Greg was shopping with his girlfriend. But he was very cold to his old teacher. After a few perfunctory words, Greg told his girlfriend, "I'll be waiting for you outside."

Mr. Morrison turned awkwardly to the girlfriend, saying, "I was his sixth grade teacher."

"I know who you are," she said. "Greg really looked up to you, but now he hates you for not caring about or even talking to him about his mother's death."

Mr. Morrison learned the hard way that it is the adult's job to start the conversation. A friend can simply say, "I'm so sorry this happened." A family member can ask, "Is there anything you want to know about your mom dying?"

Sometimes the one person with whom a child could most easily discuss his personal feelings is the one who died. You can let the child know that it's okay to talk about it, but it's also okay not to talk about it, that you'll be there when he's ready. Children will let you know whether or not they're ready if you make yourself available to them, and when they've had enough, they'll let you know that too. They will probably want to change the subject or leave. If they appear engaged and ask questions, keep talking in an age-appropriate manner. Children, unlike adults, don't stop and give you their full attention. They may be fiddling with something while you talk, but don't mistake this for not listening or caring.

Children take words literally, so we must speak concretely and not be surprised by their questions. Younger children tend to ask about the physicality of death: "Where is the body?" "How do they eat when they are buried?" "When will they wake up?" Left unattended, these questions can lead to confusion. To a four-year-old, don't be surprised if you find yourself answering questions about whether someone is "totally" dead or only "partly" dead. Do they still eat, breathe, walk, and talk? You need to be very clear.

A teacher attempted to use the following explanation: "Death is when your body stops working," he said. "Then it is dead."

A little girl in the class pointed to a boy in a wheelchair. "Tommy's legs don't work anymore. They must be dead, so how come he doesn't bury them?"

Words carry emotions and have unimagined consequences. For instance, in describing cremation, you might say that the body goes into a heated metal box rather than describing it as an "oven." It *is* an oven, but since we have ovens in our kitchens in which we prepare our meals, try to avoid the emotional association. Say, "The body is heated until it turns to ash" rather than "burned." Some children can be traumatized to learn that their favorite aunt is about to be burned. The child may think, "Wasn't dying bad enough—now we have to burn her too?"

Even a seemingly simple statement like "Mom went to heaven" can be misinterpreted. "Why can't we take a drive there and bring her back?" the child might ask. Or "Why did she choose heaven over us? Doesn't she love us anymore?" A seven-year-old boy's father told him that death was really called the Grim Reaper and was a Halloween character. Old people, he explained, couldn't run fast enough to get away from the Grim Reaper, which is why Grandpa died. The child never enjoyed Halloween again.

Children's counselors have insightful stories to tell about their clients. Emily's parents sat her down to explain that Grandpa would soon die. The six-year-old had many questions. "Can we still visit him and make popcorn?" "Will he spend lots of time with the other dead people?" "How will we know when he's dead for sure?"

Her parents answered every question with patience and compassion—until she asked, "When do they chop off his head?"

The parents were taken aback and said, "Honey, no one chops off his head. He just dies."

"So *after* he dies," she said quite earnestly, "then do they chop off his head?"

Her stunned parents answered abruptly, "There is no chopping off of heads!"

After the funeral, Emily and her grandmother were alone in the kitchen when her grandmother asked, "Emily, how are you doing? Do you have any questions about your grandpa dying?"

Emily hesitated and then she said, "Do you promise not to get mad like Mom and Dad did?"

Grandma nodded and Emily asked her question again. "When do they chop off his head?

"Where in the world did you ever get such an idea?" Grandma asked.

"Remember when we visited *your* mom at the cemetery," said Emily, "and you showed me her 'head' stone. Isn't that where they keep the head—inside the stone?"

Emily's grandmother quickly cleared up the misunderstanding.

Children respond in different ways after a loss. When a child's grades fall, adults may consider that the child is not doing so well. But a lack of attention in school after a death, or any reaction at all, is a normal sign. A child *should* be affected by loss. Grades may decline, children may keep to themselves more than before, or they may reject playing games they previously loved and excelled in. These are normal reactions, and no reaction at all may be unseen or delayed grief.

Not every child's grades will drop and there might not be significant school problems after a death. Children will deal with it in their own time, since grief has a fail-safe mechanism that will hold the loss intact until a child is old enough or psychologically prepared enough to deal with it. However, when grief occurs naturally within them, that is fine, and more often than not, talking about death will not harm a child. Protecting them from it will not necessarily protect them in life. We need to take our cues from children and, if necessary, face them head-on.

Franklin, a fifty-six-year-old electrician, recalled his own childhood experience. "They told me my grandmother had 'gone to sleep,'" he says, "but no one would tell me when she was going to wake up. They left me in the car at her funeral, and even though I was only five, I remember every detail perfectly. 'It's better for you,' they told me. 'You'll understand later.'

"All I understood was that death was a horrible thing and I never got to say good-bye to my grandmother. How did they expect me to learn that death is a normal part of life if they kept hiding it from me? I don't blame them. They did what they thought was right. But maybe if they hadn't treated death like such a horrible thing I wouldn't be so terrified of it today. I can't even go to the cemetery to visit my mother's grave. And anything to do with death or dying or being dead scares the hell out of me. I want my children to have a better understanding. When I go, I know my kids will feel sad, but I don't want them to feel unsettled and unable to feel their pain."

Franklin's childhood experiences motivated him to do it differently when he was eventually faced with his own terminal illness. He decided he wanted to continue on in his daughter's life in a tangible way after he was gone, so before he was permanently confined to bed, he made several videotapes of himself. The first was for when she started dating, the second when she began college, a third for when she was about to get married, a fourth when she became a parent, and one more for when she just missed him.

In that last one he tells her, "I know if you're watching this tape you're probably missing me. You may wonder if I miss you too. I can tell you that I do. I want you to know that the hardest thing for me in dying was leaving you behind. I tried and tried and tried not to leave you, and in the end I had to go. I know you will think of me often, as I will of you. On those days when you're busy in your life at school or with friends, and out of the blue I pop into your mind for no reason, just know that at that moment I'm thinking of you. There will be times in your life when you may feel lonely, but you will never be alone. I will always be as close as your heart."

Videotapes and video cameras are a powerful new tool in coping with loss, the ramifications of which are just beginning to be known. A simple letter can also mean the world to a child in grief.

We hope that the words we leave our children will continue to comfort them, that they will be symbolic of how we lived and how we died. The teaching we do now will help shape our children's perceptions of loss, which will affect many generations to come. We spend a great deal of time teaching our children about life, and when someone is dying, we have a profound opportunity to teach them how to care for loved ones in their last days. We can also teach them to build a healthy belief system around death and loss. We can show them ways to honor the memory of loved ones who have died, rather than leave them with unsolved mysteries.

A school nurse once got permission to take a group of high school students from her church to the cemetery to learn about death and grief. She explained to them how to visit the grave to pay respect to the person who died. She talked about spending time talking to them and sharing with them. She mentioned that bringing flowers was a nice way to show respect and offer something beautiful to someone after they were gone.

Then she gave them an assignment. "First find the oldest person in the cemetery," she said. "Then find the youngest." Her students were shocked to find a grave for a baby who died at birth. When they found the grave closest to their own age, this became a jumping-off point for them to talk in a deeper way about God and the meaning of life and death.

Children aren't the only ones who have misunderstandings about death, and sometimes they inadvertently teach the adults. Jenny was six years old when her beloved grandfather died at home. Her mother had done a wonderful job preparing her during his illness, and when he finally passed away, Jenny's mother told her she could say good-bye and hold Grandpa's hand one last time if she wanted.

Jenny approached the body of her grandpa without hesitation. In fact she looked like a scientist on an exploration. She touched his hand, and then she lifted up his arm and gently let it fall. She then started poking at him as if to make sure he was really dead. Jenny's mom became a bit alarmed, and then Jenny suddenly ran out of the room. Her mom decided to just give Jenny a few minutes before checking on her. When the young girl reappeared at her grandfather's body and started poking him again, her mother became upset and was ready to snap at her to stop. Before she could say anything, Jenny reached over her grandfather and stuck a crumpled piece of paper in his pajama pocket. Then she left the room again.

Her mother, a bit angry by now, removed the paper and was about to lecture her little girl on how to treat a loved one who has passed, when she realized it was a note. The childish printing read, "God, please take good care of my grandpa." Jenny's mom realized that the child was not being rough with the body of her grandfather. Rather, she was making sure he was dead before sending him to God with instructions.

Children often take on a heightened sense of responsibility when a loved one dies, but it isn't always expressed so positively. They often think the death is their fault, not a result of something else that happened.

Tina, for example, was thrilled that her grandmother was visiting for a month. On the first night they sat together and giggled at everything. She loved reading jokes out of a kids' joke book, and her grandmother went back and forth between "Tell me another" and "Stop! I can't take any more."

The next morning when her grandma had a heart attack, Tina remembered Grandma holding her chest and saying, "Stop! I can't take any more." Tina was sure she had killed her grandmother with too many jokes. Thirty years later, Tina's mother told her that high blood pressure and cholesterol ran in the family. "Look at Grandma," her mother said. "She never took her blood pressure pills or ate right. She had terrible heart disease for years and died of a heart attack when she was visiting. Do you remember?"

Tina looked at her mother with tear-filled eyes. "I always thought I killed her by making her laugh too hard." As Tina spoke the words out loud, it finally dawned on her that she could not have caused the death of her grandmother by making her laugh. The child inside of her was integrated into the adult at that moment.

A child who experiences a death of a loved one loses her innocence quickly. She learns that life doesn't hold guarantees, and that makes her feel like she can't count on anything.

How a child deals with news of death is as individual as the child. One ten-year-old boy was discussing his mother, who had died recently. He said, "She had a long life, she lived to forty-one years old."

Public funerals can be great lessons. Ronald Reagan's state funeral was an opportunity for this generation to teach their kids about taking time to grieve and to understand history. The fact that a funeral motorcade never travels faster than twenty miles per hour sends a message that with death, we should not rush.

Bereavement groups can help children enormously, especially when they feel isolated in their loss. In a group, you don't have to explain much, like why you are there. The reason is established the minute you walk through the door.

In the end, whether we tell our children ourselves, or encourage them to see counselors or join groups, our words and actions are always doing the teaching for us. We hope that the grief our children witness and experience will not be forgotten or considered meaningless. Rather, we want our actions around grief and death to symbolize to our kids how we lived. It is through these actions that we will help shape our children's future and will affect many generations to come.

We spend so much time teaching our children about life, why not do the same with death?

MULTIPLE LOSSES

Can you imagine losing more than one loved one at a time? Or in the midst of your grief about your loved one, a second loved one dies? It's hard to imagine, but for some, this is their tragic reality.

Marsha, Dean, and their three kids had tickets for the last game of the baseball season. The day before the game, Marsha's boss called and said he desperately needed her to work on Saturday. Since he had always been more than generous with her, Marsha decided to forgo the game and help out her boss. And since her brother was jealous that they had tickets to a sold-out game, she called him and offered the ticket, which he accepted with great joy.

The score was tied for most of the game, and in the bottom of the last inning the home team won. Dean called Marsha at work and told her how great the game had been; they would pick her up and they would all go celebrate.

On their way to get Marsha, everyone was crammed in the car with the ice chest in back. Joey, their four-year-old, handed his father a drink. Apparently he remembered how much fun they'd had just the day before shaking cans and squirting them at each other. Before he gave the drink to his dad, he shook it up. When Dean opened the can, it exploded in his face, causing him to lose control of the car and careen over the embankment. Dean and two of the kids were killed on impact. As Joey was wheeled into emergency surgery at the hospital, he kept telling everyone the story and was concerned about how much trouble he would be in for shaking the soda. Because of internal hemorrhaging he did not survive the surgery.

Marsha was left to deal with unbelievable losses. In the midst of her shock and grief, she had to arrange the funerals of her husband, her two sons, her daughter, and her brother.

In multiple losses such as this tragedy, the shock lasts much longer. The denial is much stronger. The anger is more intense and the sadness and depression deeper. As long as Marsha was concerned with the larger overwhelming tragedy, it would be difficult for her to mourn all her loved ones individually. But once she dealt with the trauma and got through the shock and denial, it was important for her literally to separate out each loss.

If Marsha started to mourn her husband and then got bombarded with feelings of loss for her children and then her brother, she only sank deeper into the loss. Instead, when she felt ready, she took a day or even a week to focus on her husband alone. She went through old photographs, visited places that had meaning to their marriage, lit a candle for him, and spoke to him. Then she did the same for each of her three children and her brother, remembering and honoring each one individually.

In these cases it becomes hard to know whom you are grieving at any given moment. The losses all naturally meld together on their own. But it is important to give each person his or her due. In Marsha's situation, we would imagine that over time, she would do many intermittent weeks for her husband, her children, and her family. The first time, she might organize one week for each. After that it would occur much more organically.

It is not necessary to do it this way, but it is important to note that if you are constantly grieving for one person and the others intrude on that grief, you will continually feel overwhelmed by that grief. If this happens, compartmentalizing can be very helpful for separating out all the losses. In most cases we would suggest professional help or support groups whenever possible since there are so many emotions to sort through, not to mention such things as the planning of the funerals and figuring out financial solutions to handle the expenses. And there may be legal logistics if the death was caused by an accident.

Many people spend time in the anger stage or the "why me?" stage. They often ask irrational questions, such as "Why did I ever let them go to the game?" "Why did I ask him to go out and get some bread? I could have waited."

You must give yourself a break. You "let" them go to the game because life is for living and baseball games are part of life. So is grocery shopping. The what ifs of bargaining will never result in a different outcome. Life is inherently risky, no matter how careful we are. But even though these questions do not produce answers, it is normal to examine these issues and pursue them in our minds. In fact, we must ask these questions before we can move on to other levels of grief.

Another kind of multiple-loss situation is when a loved one has died while you are still mourning the loss of someone else.

Edith was concerned and thankful when both her sons were on the battlefront in Vietnam, since one son, James, was twenty-two and would be able to watch over her baby, Andy, who was only eighteen. Her husband was a pilot, and both boys followed in their father's footsteps. They both ended up piloting Huey helicopters, transporting fresh troops into combat and returning with casualties. On one mission, James landed unknowingly in a minefield. As troops disembarked one soldier stepped on and exploded a land mine.

James was a flight leader, and Andy was flying one of the other helicopters that was part of the team. James was hit by shrapnel through the hull of his chopper. Word spread instantaneously that the lead pilot was hit and his door would not open. Andy ran over to James's helicopter in spite of the threat of land mines and tried to rescue his severely injured older brother. Andy succeeded in opening the door and getting his brother to another chopper. As Andy jumped in for a quick departure, he was shot and killed. Edith was devastated. She counted the days until James would be well enough to leave the field infirmary and return home. Edith and her husband longed for James to be home to share their mutual grief.

Edith was in deep mourning and yet was so very thankful when the week came that her surviving son would be well enough for transport back to the United States. On the day before his flight home, the field infirmary was bombed and James was killed. Edith and her husband, still raw with grief from the loss of Andy, now faced the sad mourning of their first son, James.

There are many other examples of multiple losses, such as accidents, epidemics like AIDS, school shootings, or any other situation when we lose more than one loved one in close succession.

When we are hit with multiple losses because of illness, we may wonder who is next. Many times people feel unsafe if they belong to a group that is affected by an epidemic. If a workplace suffers a number of deaths from cancer, employees may wonder if there is a reason. Maybe it's environmental, they think, or "Maybe this place is cursed." That is our way of trying to understand and give meaning to something that seems to have none. The same feelings may arise when multiple deaths occur in one family.

"Why was I spared?" is an often-asked question. "Why didn't I die instead of my child or my wife?" This reaction, another form of survivor's guilt, is an intensely felt guilt. "Why them and not me?" The phenomenon of survivor's guilt also occurs when many die and some are spared.

Some even call it arrogance to ask "Why not me?" Only

after we have worked through the grief are we able to understand that it is not up to us. Who lives and who dies are decisions for God and the Universe to make. Ultimately, every survivor has to move on from wondering why to figuring out what to do with the rest of their life.

You will feel as if you can never really live again, that your life will never be the same and neither will you. But in the years to come, you will find ways to live with your losses. Your grief may be delayed, but that comes with this tragic territory. Some even go on to find new meaning or purpose in life after these losses. Just give yourself plenty of time and reach out for help. It may take years, but in time you will find a way to honor the lives that were lost, without the excruciating pain you feel at this moment.

DISASTERS

Disasters are clearly a natural occurrence of nature and the Universe—until they happen to you and your loved ones. Any death can be considered a disaster, because it devastates our life. But disasters that result in mass casualties can be natural events (earthquakes, floods, wildfires, tsunamis, hurricanes, etc.), technological events (toxic spills, transportation accidents, chemical explosions, etc.), or man-made or deliberately caused (violence, sabotage, terrorism, arson, civil unrest, etc.).

Although very different in origin, these disasters are similar in that they often cause large numbers of deaths and injuries and wide paths of destruction in a community. Homes can be destroyed and neighborhoods wiped out. Individuals lose personal belongings as well as loved ones. Personal and community grief are combined. Survivors are exposed to horrible sights, sounds and smells. And if the disaster is man-made or deliberately caused, sorrow is interspersed with intense anger as survivors mourn their losses and rail at the perpetrator who killed their loved one needlessly.

In the world of disasters, we move from normal human experiences to a realm outside them. We have no foundation to prepare us to watch someone burn up in flames or hear large numbers of people crying out as they die. As a survivor, you feel that you and only you enter this new, unwanted world.

A wife watched her husband burn up in the seat beside her in an airline crash. She witnessed many others die in the flames that engulfed the fuselage, while for whatever reason, she survived physically unharmed. Walking away while others perish is beyond most people's comprehension, but, a few days after the crash, the wife was on another flight going home with her loved one in a casket in the cargo hold. Some may ask how she ever felt safe on an airplane again. For her, however, the question was much larger: how would she ever feel safe in the *world* again? She realized that she might not.

If you are left feeling unsafe in your own world, we encourage you to take advantage of any help offered. You must deal with the trauma itself before you can deal with the grief. Trauma may result in Post-Traumatic Stress Disorder (PTSD), a reaction to an event outside the normal realm of human experience, when the trauma from a shocking and painful event slows down the grief reaction. PTSD is an emotional disorder in which a person suffers from re-experiencing the horrific event through hyperarousal and extreme anxiety; intrusive thoughts and memories, or flashbacks; and emotional numbing. It is as if a videotape of the event is stuck in playback mode.

In grief, a person can usually talk about how their loved one was diagnosed, then became sicker, then died. All the events, no matter how sad, are available for recollection in the order that they occurred. This kind of memory is linear. When trauma occurs, however, there are often blank spaces, things you can't recall, parts of the story that are too painful for the conscious mind to remember.

Sometimes in disasters we are faced with trauma, death, and survival all mixed together. Jane was new to living on the Gulf Coast. She loved the South and enjoyed her large apartment complex just blocks from the water. She lived through many hurricanes and felt a sense of excitement about them, but she had never been through one that did any damage.

One day, when a hurricane was headed toward the coast, she decided to stay in her apartment with friends, just as she had done with the other hurricanes so common to where she lived. There was something about being together and weathering the storm that felt satisfying and safe.

The night began like the others, with lots of rain and wind. But suddenly things began to change and the windows started to break. Everyone quickly moved into other rooms, shoving the furniture into the center of the room to protect it. When the lights went out, they lit candles and stared at each other through the eerie glow. There was a danger present that none of them had felt before.

At the point when they realized they had to leave the apartment, located on the third story of the building, they walked out the door in a line holding hands. The walkway was covered in water, not only from the rain but also the tides that were washing up the shore—farther than ever before.

They felt panic rising when a few stragglers went back into the apartment, and Jane led the rest up to the roof. From there, she lost track of all that happened. She was a good swimmer and decided to make her descent from the roof. She remembers hanging on to bushes. She thinks at one point she clutched a branch, not realizing it was only a treetop. The voices of her friends disappeared as she fell into the water below and got carried out to sea. Now she began the fight of her life as she tried to swim toward shore.

It was difficult to sense in which direction she was heading, but she swam for hours, fearing she would certainly die in the middle of the Gulf. Somehow, with many blank spots in her memory of the long night, she finally reached the shore, grabbing onto a building. The sun came up over the wet devastation, and when she made her way down from the building, she was standing in the northern part of her city, which meant she had swum for three miles while her home was completely underwater.

The complexities of healing from this single horrific night will take Jane a lifetime. From the loss of her home to being one of the few survivors in her building, the death, destruction, and the struggle for life have created an entanglement of grief and trauma.

Deaths in disasters can be like no other. The number of dead can be overwhelming, like in the Southeast Asian tsunami of 2004. Taking care of the bodies can be a community crisis. Surviving family members may be confronted with severely damaged bodies of their loved ones. Issues may arise around prolonged recovery or identification. Or, there may be no body at all, which presents emotional challenges for which most survivors are unprepared.

Survivors mourn losses after the disaster on multiple levels— their loved one is gone, their home and neighborhood is disrupted, their sense of safety is violated. Oftentimes the disaster invites the world community into their backyards as witnesses. They are forced into interaction with multiple levels of bureaucracy: local, state, and federal disaster recovery agencies. News media from around the world broadcast the tragedy for everyone to see, hear, and read about. Mourning becomes public.

The collective grief and anger over a disaster often results in bonding with strangers who have undergone a similar loss. It is hard being showered with help and questions while in the midst of a loss, only to find that within weeks, your loved ones are gone forever and the rest of the world has moved on to a new disaster.

The details of disasters are usually devastating and must be teased out to begin the process of moving through the trauma and loss as we wonder why we survived. Still, as much as we take precautions, we cannot avoid natural disasters.

A woman who lived in Los Angeles experienced a minor earthquake. It scared her so much that she decided that it was too risky to live in an earthquake-prone area. She moved to Kauai in the Hawaiian Islands, where she felt much more safe and at peace. But literally three weeks later, Hurricane Iniki struck and devastated the entire island. She had to stand in line to use a phone, her food and water were rationed, and because she now lived on a remote island, it was a very long time before the roads and toppled buildings were repaired. She felt as if there were no safety anywhere in this world, but she came to understand that her choice was not responsible for inviting the disaster that occurred.

Man-made disasters like the Madrid train bombings, the Pan Am explosion over Lockerbie, the sarin nerve agent release in the Tokyo subway, and the September 11, 2001, World Trade Center terrorist acts, catapult survivors into a very public and prolonged grappling with the disaster on multiple levels. There is intense media coverage on their community. Everyone who was not there wants to know what it was like. And as the perpetrators are hunted and tracked, anxiety and involvement with the disaster remains high for the survivors. If the perpetrators are caught, then comes more media, years of legal wrangling as things come to trial, weeks or months of the trial itself, then the verdict. All of this forces the survivor back into the memories, back into the grief, back into the mourning.

If you lost a loved one in a disaster, the stage of denial may be greater, since we all think that disasters will never happen to us. We may be very angry that our loved one was in the disaster and not someone else. Or we may be angry at Mother Nature, that her "fury" entered our world.

Many take pilgrimages yearly to visit a loved one. If you lost yours in an airline disaster in the ocean, you can visit the closest shore, or go out on a boat to have a yearly memorial. A woman told us that when her daughter died in a plane crash, she had so much grief, she kept returning to the crash site to grieve a little more and help herself make the loss real.

Many families involved in disasters take yearly visits to the area of loss and find these group rituals to be a great help. They gather to support each other in an event that no one else can understand. If the area where your loved one died is not readily available for a visit, though, you can visit the loss in your mind from time to time. These kinds of mental visits are greatly helpful in acceptance and acknowledgment of the loss and tragedy.

We may not think we will survive the loss and devastation of a disaster, but even if you can't see it for some time, even if you wonder how there can ever be life again after such trauma, you do have more life left. We are more resilient than we know. Everyone thought that after 9/11 New York would be a city of terribly traumatized people unable to function. That has not been the case. Trauma invites us to learn about our strength, endurance, and hope after it visits.

A tree that has been cut down has experienced physical

trauma. One would think its life completely over. But then a small sprout of life comes out, very slowly and very quietly.

SUICIDE

An actual suicide note, reprinted with the permission of the survivors.

Dear Mom, Dad, and Gregory,

If I am successful and can go through with it this time, I want you to know I am really sorry, but I have no more hope for myself and I feel so stuck in the deepest of ruts. I want to free myself from all this misery I've put upon myself. I have forever lost myself, my soul, and my existence for who I am and my purpose in life. I don't know what is right anymore.

I am worn from thinking so negatively and being unable to relinquish myself from this torture. I feel so much fear around others. I've thought of lots of ways to kill myself yet always think about you guys, mom, dad, and Gregory and have really been fighting it with everything I have. Sometimes I think there is hope for me but then I start doubting myself. I know this seems like the weakest of things to do and it probably is, yet I really feel damaged and it's nobody's fault but mine. I am so sorry for all that I am putting you all through, something that is so unfair and not really respectable, but I am weak and I don't think I'd make it. I'm hoping if I go through with this God will understand. The worst loss to me is you guys, my family, and yet I don't know any other way to make it better. I feel so sick for all, but I can't change this feeling inside my head. I am so sorry mom. I love all of you. Its just time for me to rise above this planet and free my soul from the torture I'm putting on it and have put upon you. I wish I could describe what I feel inside, the anger, the pain and my inability to connect with it or to make it better.

Love is all I wanted. At least this is what I feel like now and I don't have love within anymore. I have terror of myself as not being the loving person that I am. It's not me. I don't even know me anymore. I tried and this is nobody's fault but my own. Yet if I could show you how much I love all of you, I promise I will, just not in this matter. I will do it in spirit. I hope God looks after me and I hope He understands and forgives me. I am going to miss you so much that I want to stay and work out these problems. I can't do this. I can't stop the flow of energy but God there is just no help anymore. I feel stuck. I'm so upset that I have not done anything in life. I feel totally academically incapable. I am sorry and I love all of you. Please forgive me. It was not any of you. It is all me.

Love,

Robert

The above is an actual letter, and Robert was able to go through with it that time. His letter illustrates so many of the dynamics that go into a suicide. You can clearly see his struggle with life and his sense of failure and disappointment that life was not going the way he wanted it to. You can hear the loss of hope, often a theme that runs through the siren call to suicide. The individual does not want death, but they do want out of the pain. Robert battled his own mind day in and day out to stay alive. He had a glimpse of the person he wanted to be, but he could not get there. He even let his loved ones know that this was not their fault.

Even though this letter explained his struggles and released his family from responsibility, it brought them little comfort. In survivor after suicide groups there is often a discussion about whether it is better to have found a note or not. For some it is irrelevant, because in the big picture the person you cared about is gone. Those who did not receive a note wish desperately for any clue into their loved one's psyche. Those who are left with notes find them lacking answers, or find that the answers are too late to act upon. For the latter group they are left with an added frustration that acting upon the information might have changed the outcome. In many cases, though, the information has already been verbalized in bits and pieces.

Grief over a loved one's suicide is its own type of grief. There is a sense of guilt and anger, but also shame. Families are left with a feeling of enormous stigma around the suicide, and so, few talk about it. Some make up false reasons to explain their loved one's death, since shame is part of the guilt. Guilt is the feeling of self-judgment, the sense that we have done something wrong, and that sense strengthens when we think we might have contributed to someone's death, even if it was by refusal to listen and take their pain seriously. Guilt is anger turned inward, arising when we violate our belief systems—"Everyone can be saved"— or those in which we were raised: "Other people take their own lives, not our family or friends." Guilt is part of the human experience, and in order to move past it, we must align our beliefs and our actions. Could we really have saved someone? If we did more, would it really have made a difference?

While guilt is about what you think you did, shame is about who you think you are. Maybe you think that a loved one would rather die than be with you one more day. As a mother once asked us, "Could anything cause you more social shame than having a suicide forever brand your family as dysfunctional?" While guilt attacks your consciousness, shame assaults your soul.

After suicide, loved ones may experience their own sense of hopelessness. Oftentimes they need to find any glimmer of hope or have a loved one help find it for them. The survivors may feel isolated and cut off from everyone, compounded with the guilt they may feel. When this occurs, they tend to pull away and shut down.

Erin dealt with her husband's suicidal thoughts for years. Ray was a highly functioning, bright man who looked very healthy, but in truth, he was on medication to help even out a chemical imbalance in his brain. Over the years he appeared to have ups and downs, like everyone else, and Erin struggled during his tough times. She constantly feared he would make good his threat to end his life.

It seemed that his therapist and his physician were helping him keep his dark thoughts at bay, but in the end, nothing worked and he completed suicide. Erin was stunned, even though she had heard him speak of it so many times. "He seemed to be doing well, and then out of the blue he goes and kills himself!"

Often, a strange phenomenon occurs a few days before a suicide when someone announces to friends and family that they've never felt better. Erin learned after the fact that such an announcement can be an omen, rather than a sign of healing, because the person has come to a decision in their mind. They have decided to die, and therefore the stressors of their lives have become irrelevant. In Ray's case, Erin said, "The near suicides were bad, but what was I supposed to do—consider every improvement a possible suicide? Does this mean that every bit of his happiness was a secret sign that he had a plan? After a year or two of his threats, I couldn't live my life that way."

Erin was not just a witness to her husband's pain but, in many ways, made it *their* struggle. Many families do this; how can you *not* become part of the struggle if your son, daughter, or other loved one is thinking of killing themself?

Suicide eliminates all sense of well-being within a family. You may even feel betrayed. How did she do this without letting you know? How did she take the very battle that the two of you were fighting together, and end it without you? The anger may be overwhelming, because the act of suicide is a horrendous blow beyond that of the death. To lose a loved one through suicide can feel like a brutal slap in the face. We are left with feelings of loss, betrayal, and abandonment.

We know from some people who have decided to end their lives and didn't complete the act that they felt relieved and grateful. They can see that life was not the problem, but the pain was. They wanted to stop the pain, they had lost hope in finding an alternative, and they decided there was no other answer to their struggles. As each possibility drops away into ineffectiveness, ending life is the only remaining solution.

It has been said that if the dying take their own life, they will still have to learn the lessons they were supposed to learn in life. It seems that the enormous pain they had in life may follow them into death. And a tragic life may teach those left behind some important lessons, such as the need for more kindness in the world. Sometimes a lesson may be hard to find amid the pain and loss.

Katie was a loving, energetic woman in her midthirties who loved life and longed for happiness. When she was six and her parents divorced, her father got custody and he began sexually abusing her. After a year of unspeakable abuse, she got up the courage to tell her mother and a few other adults, but no one believed her. The abuse continued into her teenage years until she ran away from her father when she was sixteen.

In her early twenties, it seemed as if she was finally having a normal life, but her childhood came back to haunt her. She turned to drugs to numb the memories, and she was in and out of rehab until her midthirties, when she became determined to make her life work. She went to twelve-step meetings, attended church, and volunteered in community service organizations, but the demons from her past always seemed to follow her. Onlookers could see her radiance, but at the same time, they could feel the sad undercurrents of her childhood trauma. When she died by her own hand at the age of thirty-seven, her friends grieved, but the ones who knew her well were also glad she was free of pain.

Survivors may feel relief that their loved one's unworkable life is over and that the person is no longer struggling. After a time, they may feel guilty for thinking that their loved one's death is better than their life of pain. It is important for the survivor to remember, however, that there are always other alternatives, other solutions, even though their loved one was not able to see them.

Survivors, at some phase of their own grief, may feel suicidal themselves as they go through the grief process. The pain of the loss may be felt as too great to handle and the survivor may just want to give up and go where the loved one is. These feelings can be frightening, but usually they pass. The best way to understand this phase is to seek professional help from a person familiar with the process of grief from a suicidal loss.

If this sounds familiar, we suggest that you seek professional support. Survivor after suicide groups can be very helpful as you spend time with others in the same kind of pain. But not only family members are devastated. A psychologist who specializes in suicide shared, "The last patient who died by her own hands while under my watch was in a terribly dark place. I vowed to save her, but I couldn't, and that death has been with me for a long time. I may have skills to help people through a suicidal depression, but I have to remember that I'm not God. There are things over which I have no control."

Loved ones are left with an enormous sense of responsibility after suicide. Jenny and Vanessa were college roommates. They shared a phone, and one day one of Vanessa's friends, Keith, called. Jenny had met Keith once and knew his voice, but when he called for Vanessa, Jenny was busy with her studies and simply said, "She's not in, but I'll tell her you called."

Later, when Jenny found out that Keith had died by suicide that day, she was tortured with the thought that she could at least have asked how he was. If strangers feel this way about someone's suicide, you can understand the huge responsibility with which close loved ones are left.

Healing after a loved one's suicide is complicated; before you work through the grief, you must first work through the guilt. You must come to the place where you understand logically that you are *not* responsible for someone else's taking their own life. Then you will gradually come to forgive both yourself and your loved one. You will need to find a space inside of you to be sad and sorry and to build a new relationship with your loved one without clinging to how the person died or defining their life by their death.

People who would benefit from working through that transition often remain stuck, unintentionally causing emotional damage to themselves and their relationships. In the strangest of ironies, they may end up sometimes thinking, "I don't feel like going on." They feel they should have understood the warning signs, but maybe there was an argument, denial, or something else that got in the way of their seeing it coming.

Social isolation is a huge danger in suicide, because it produces the kind of grief we don't often share. We alone are left with part of their pain as well as our own. This isolation leads to a lack of the very support systems that may be so helpful to your healing.

One Thursday night a few college students were sitting around the dorm watching TV together. The program showed a teenager struggling to read a note from his mother, fearing she would blame him for her demise. When he got up the nerve to read the handwritten note, it said that she loved him very much and he was the best part of her life. The teenager felt whole again knowing that he was not the reason for his mother's death and that she loved him very much.

The students were fairly quiet until the note was read and Tom, a senior, startled the group when he yelled "Liar!" at the TV. The other kids questioned him about his reaction and he explained, "If she loved him, she wouldn't have killed herself."

What the group didn't know was that Tom was speaking from experience. He had lost his own mother to suicide. "Yeah," he said sarcastically, "now that the kid got the note telling him it wasn't his fault, everything is just fine." Tom knew this was TV, not real life.

Real notes and real lives are harder to deal with, as Tom shared when he started talking about his sorrow with his friends. He told them, "One of the hardest parts of the grief is that people don't know what to say to us. They're afraid to say the wrong thing, but it really makes no difference how someone died. People can just say, 'I'm sorry your mother died.' "

Family members are not sure if they are going to be okay when it comes to handling a suicide. There are no models for it, and the loss can become multigenerational. If you lost your adult brother to suicide, you worry about his kids and yours. You also worry about your parents, who have to endure the loss of a child. If you don't share the truth about the suicide in the family, you will end up increasing the shame and secrecy. You may also experience the trauma of discovering a loved one's body—a terrible image to carry around for the rest of your life. Or you may find the stigma of suicide played out when certain clergy members will not participate in the funeral service.

Eloise, who lost her sister to suicide, says that the comments hurt more than people think, such as "Oh no, not your sister, Vivian. I had no idea she was that messed up." Even comments that aren't personal can hurt to the quick, making it tough to live with our shame in society. Think about offhanded comments such as "I would rather kill myself than do that," or "If I had to live there, I would slit my wrists." All of those expressions, like "Just shoot me," or "Take a flying leap off a cliff," take on a deeper meaning when you have lost someone to suicide.

We cannot stress enough that suicide survivors need as much support as anyone else in grief. If you can't find a survivor after suicide group available, you can join a regular bereavement group. The main difference between you and the others in grief is that most likely, their loved one died of a disease or old age, while your story is about someone who orchestrated his own death. But in the end, you are all feeling grief, and it is better than having no group at all and subsequently isolating yourself.

We already spoke about receiving suicide notes from loved ones, but we also see that writing your own note to someone who killed themself can be helpful.

My Dear Willie

As you hear me read this letter to you, I would like you to know that I miss you and that so much has changed because of you. I always thought this sort of thing happened to other people, not to us. Maybe in your heart you thought you were doing me favor by taking your own life. What hurts most is that you never really said good-bye or gave me a chance to say good-bye to you. My eyes have cried a million tears as I have tried to change what has happened, trying to understand your pain, your desperation, your misery.

At times I have been angry with you for what you did to yourself and for what you did to me. At times I felt responsible for your death. I've searched for what I did or failed to do for any possible clue I missed. Yet I also know that no matter what, I couldn't choose for you. I am learning to stop feeling responsible for your death; if I were responsible for you and your life, you'd still be alive.

I think of you so often, even when it hurts to remember. Whenever I hear your songs, I still cry for you. I feel sad that you're not here to share so many wonderful events with me. Slowly, though, it's getting easier. I am beginning to remember the good times. Maybe you've seen me smiling again. Yes, I am learning to live again and have decided that I will not die because you chose to die. I pray that you have now found the peace that you were looking for. I believe that you are at peace. I forgive you for this and for whatever else has happened during our time together. Most importantly I have forgiven myself for any pain that I believe I may have caused you, because I know that you are forgiving me in the divinity of heaven and God's love, compassion, and mercy. At the end of my days, I look forward to being with you again.

I will always love and remember you as my sweetheart.

Tina

ALZHEIMERS DISEASE

Mary, an active woman in her sixties, said, "The grief didn't begin when my husband died. It began the day my worst suspicions were confirmed that Kevin had Alzheimers. I was losing my husband piece by piece. I was losing the personality of the person I knew and loved. In so many ways, we are our memories. Now, all those wonderful bits of memories, all those sacred things we shared were disappearing like tears in rain."

There is no easy way to say good-bye to someone you love. The slow process of losing the personality of someone dear while they remain physically intact is devastating as well as unsettling. You wonder what she is going through as her memories seem to be replaced with a black hole of nothingness. Where is she? What does she feel and think? Who is it that lives on after the personality dies?

Ellen's mother was diagnosed with Alzheimers after she'd lost much of her memory. As her mother's personality changed, Ellen said, "Some people think it is like being under stress, when the worst parts of your personality come out. They are suggesting that a slightly angry person might become permanently enraged or abusively mean. But it isn't like that. It's more like a brand-new personality emerges. You see, my mother was never mean or angry, but that's how she became when the Alzheimers progressed. I promised never to put her in a facility, but I had no idea how bad it could get."

Ellen had underestimated the devastation of Alzheimers. She'd pictured feeding and caring for her mother as she got sicker. She knew her mother had been depressed in her life and was prepared for it to get worse. And it did. She was prepared for someday finding her mother didn't know her. But she was not prepared for the fact that her mother thought Ellen was trying to kill her. When they went out, Ellen had to cope with her mother's screaming to anyone who would listen that she was being kidnapped. There was no time to grieve the loss of her mother's old personality while she was so busy dealing with the problems at hand.

She continued to watch her mother slip away, devastated each time she was accused of kidnapping and abuse. Ellen and her sisters pleaded with their mother that they loved her and were there only to take care of her and give back all the love they had received. But in this cruel disease, their demonstrations of love were met only with arguments by their mother claiming that her daughters were kidnappers and killers. Ellen eventually did the inevitable and committed her mother to a facility. She visited weekly for the next few years, watching the disease progress more and more. But when her mother finally died, Ellen was over-come with guilt that she had not kept her word and had put her in a facility.

Ellen could understand intellectually that it was impossible for her to keep her promise, but her heart was broken when she did what her mother did not want. Eventually, she began to see a grief counselor to work through the loss and the guilt, until she grasped the reality that she had made the only possible choice. The truth was that her mother was better off being cared for by professionals, but that added a layer of complication to the grief that she was feeling.

Most people will agree that there is no greater test for uncon-ditional love than having a loved one with Alzheimers. Don was crushed when his wife was diagnosed, and for years he watched her cry. Previously, she lit up when he'd walk into a room, and now she acted as if she detested him. It broke his heart even though she couldn't help it. After she died, Don asked God, "Why did you take her mind? Watching a mind die is a far more horrible thing than to witness the death of her body."

There are decisions that must be grieved, and modern medicine does not make it any easier for loved ones, such as: Do you nourish your loved one by medical means when they can no longer eat or drink by themself? Do you treat curable infections that, left untreated, could be the death of a loved one with Alzheimers disease?

Modern medicine offers us no model to let go of the body after the mind has died. We are left with so many questions that plague us, no matter what decisions we make, such as, "Should I have put a tube in for artificial nutrients or should I have let Mother die of starvation?"

We need to make peace with the idea that when the body permanently stops eating, it is telling you that it is time to go.

If you fed your loved one long after they could function, you may be left wondering if that was a good choice. You may have given him more time but with no quality of life. In those cases, you must make peace with yourself that you did the best you could. Modern medicine places these dilemmas upon you. You may have felt that a simple urinary infection could easily be handled with an antibiotic, and so that was the decision you made.

Whatever you did, take comfort that you did it out of love and hope, trying to do the right thing when there was no clear right thing to do. You chose a direction in a medical world with too many mixed messages to understand what is and what is not the right decision.

Whether you lean toward aggressive treatment or a more passive approach, questioning what you did after your loved one has died is normal. Fortunately or unfortunately, though, there is some relief in the air because they are no longer suffering.

After many years of watching his wife suffer with Alzheimers, a man shared at her funeral about his loss. "I know it is poetic to say it was 'the long good-bye,' but there was nothing good in it. It was mostly confusing, and today I can only say farewell to her sad, rocky journey. I really hope she is finally at peace and whole again."

When death finally comes after a loss, you may feel you experienced your loved one's death long ago, grieving each loss along the way. Those markers of time that meant so much to both of you began to disappear: the movies, the holidays, the trips that you took. The graduations, weddings, all disappearing before your eyes. Then the day comes when your loved one does not even recognize you anymore.

How do you grieve when they are still alive? We must understand that each bit of sadness is a death in itself, a separate loss to grieve. Alzheimers gives you more than your share of losses, such as the loss of driving, the loss of independence, the loss of personality, the loss of clarity, the loss of financial control, the loss of vulnerability, the loss of a family, the loss of health, the loss of temperament, and, finally, the loss of who the person ever was.

It is death in slow motion for a couple who suffer the loss of their highly anticipated golden years. After thirty years of marriage, with whom do you reminisce? How do you live without the certainty that your spouse still loves you, when you yourself may not love who they have become? You longed for a connection. They answered your longing and now it is lost forever. In this way, their losses are yours. When they finally die, you may wonder who is actually in the casket, since the personality and spirit you knew left a long time ago.

It is a complex grief that a loved one feels after a loss to Alzheimers disease. You may feel badly that what you feel most is a sense of relief. There are also guilts, regrets, sadness, and often shame. Loved ones may have at times felt ashamed of bringing the disease into the family, as if the behaviors of someone with Alzheimers are someone's fault.

We urge you to remember that you and your family did nothing to bring this on, so you don't have to hide it. In the scheme of things, Alzheimers is still a relatively new disease, so hopefully, the more we discover about it, the less stigma it will carry.

SUDDEN DEATH

For some the call comes on an otherwise idle Thursday. For others, maybe they are overwhelmed with a weekend project when there is an unexpected knock on the door. Out of the blue our world changes when suddenly and without warning, we learn that our loved one is gone.

How can this be? They were fine and now they are not. They were here and now they are not. Death is hardest to comprehend without any forewarning. The news and loss are crushing. How can our world change so dramatically and without any warning? No preparation, no good-byes, just the loudest absence one could ever imagine. As a result, in sudden death, the denial will be longer and deeper. The suddenness thrusts us into a new, abnormal world. How can you grasp that your loved one was here for breakfast and dead by lunchtime? You can't.

In sudden death there is no time for the mind to prepare, to brace for the thunderous pain that will leave you in a severe state of shock. A mind cannot comprehend that one day, you and your wife are wondering if you should start remodeling or go on a vacation in the upcoming summer. The next day, you are deciding what kind of casket you should get to bury her. You don't grieve, because you can't yet. You are in free fall, with your grief deeply buried under your shock, trauma, and pain. It will stay there for you gradually to unearth it over several years.

Sudden death can result from illnesses, both known and unknown, as well as from an accident, a crime, or terrorism. In the case of an illness, it can come completely out of the blue. A sudden heart attack, stroke, and many other things can happen in an otherwise healthy individual or someone who is expected to recover.

For some the more sudden the death, the longer it will take to grieve the loss. The period of denial is substantially lengthened, with no chance to say good-bye and to adjust to a life without your nearest and dearest. When there is no warning, you are suddenly faced with a huge loss and a need to make funeral arrangements.

This world of loss does not give you time to let your mind or heart catch up with the world around you. The final decisions that you had no chance to discuss with your loved one may hit you like a series of blows to a boxer. Cremation or burial? What kind of casket? Who should be notified? What about the service? What did he want? What do you want for him? How can you make these kinds of decisions while you can barely accept the death as a reality? Isn't he going to walk in at any moment and end your nightmare?

Annette, a loving and caring wife in her early fifties, found it hard to think about the death of her husband, who was just two years older than she. "It's still feels so painful," she said. "People tell me to move, that my house is too large for one person. My house is like a Stradivarius violin too special to let go of. How can I explain, that would feel like I was losing Robin all over again? He was home more than I was, he was in the yard every day. I might move sometime in the future, but I can no more leave the house than stop thinking about Robin. It is a part of him, and that's hard for people to understand."

Lena's husband, Hal, was having stomach pains and bad indigestion, but he figured it was just acid reflux. The doctor suggested he have some GI testing, which he did, hoping he would feel better. After all, over the last few years, Hal had lost weight and quit smoking. When he went to bed on that fateful cool spring night, he had some bad indigestion. He was up and down all night; he even put some clothes in the dryer because he just couldn't fall asleep.

Lena knew he having a bad night, but he told her to stay in bed. When he finally came back and climbed in next to her, she asked how he was feeling.

"Maybe a little better." Lena was glad and fell back to sleep.

An hour later, a strange noise awakened Lena. "Honey," she said, "what's that sound?"

He didn't answer. "Why aren't you answering me?" she asked, gently shaking him.

"I now know that noise was death, it was a gurgling sound." Lena reached for the phone to dial 911, "but I was so upset, I dialed 411 instead."

She finally reached 911 and told the operator that her husband's eyes were rolled back in his head.

"Is he breathing?" the operator asked. "Put your ear next to his lips and listen."

She heard nothing.

"Place him on the floor," the operator directed her, quite a task for a woman as small as Lena. When the operator heard her puffing from the effort, she asked, "Is there anyone else in the house who can help you?"

"No," said Lena. "It's just us."

That was when it hit her. There was no more "us."

The paramedics arrived quickly only to confirm what she already knew, that her husband was dead.

"But he is here," she cried, "and how can he be gone? This is unbelievable."

Later she said, "You kiss your husband good night and you don't have the mental capacity to imagine that you'll be in a funeral parlor the very next morning planning his funeral. I kept thinking where was he, where did he go? I'd been with him since I was nineteen, and I kept thinking it was one of those nightmares that felt so real, you were sure you were dreaming. I kept thinking I was still sleeping and my husband was sound asleep beside me."

For the next few days following the death, Lena was in a daze as the smallest things threw her into deep sorrow and disbelief. "I was trying to just do things," she recalls, "but when I opened the dryer and there were his clothes that he put in hours before he died, I started screaming."

The sudden loss of a loved one is a particular kind of death. The sorrow of not saying good-bye hurts the most when we lose someone in the midst of a life. We wonder how it could have happened, and what we might have done to change the outcome. What if you'd arrived home earlier? What if they hadn't gone out on that errand? What if they didn't make that trip? Since most of what we do comes as a result of decisions, if we had decided to vacation sooner, would they still have died? Or what if we had returned soon enough to see the doctor? Maybe he would have survived if he was under less stress.

Shelley had a chance to explore the "what ifs" of a death. Hugh and Shelley were going on a trip to India. When they arrived at the doctor's office for shots, the receptionist asked, "Do you want to just get your shots? You're both due for a physical next month, so we can do the physicals now or when you get back." Since they were so busy preparing, Shelley decided that she would book the exams for when they returned.

The trip to India turned out to be everything they wanted it to be. After they returned home, Hugh was in the local drugstore getting the pictures developed when he had a sudden heart attack and died. For the next few months Shelley was deep in shock and grief, tortured by thinking if only they had gotten their physicals from the doctor before they left.

In order to find some peace, Shelley did a remarkable thing by making an appointment to talk to the doctor. She sat in front of him and confessed how guilty she felt for not doing the physical.

"Shelley," the doctor said, "you cannot blame yourself. Hugh looked so good when he came in, even if I'd given him a physical, I doubt I would have put him on the treadmill. His past blood work was normal, he was doing fine, and there was no way to predict this."

Shelley took some comfort in knowing that even the doctor had no clue. Of course she still had her grief, but the guilt began to dissipate, which helped her tremendously in her grieving process.

Sudden-death support groups for survivors are wonderful but few and far between. Most people have a bereavement group to go to, which, as we have mentioned, shows how universal the feelings of loss are.

One of the traps of a bereavement group is the discussion of which death was worse and who suffered more. One participant might say, "At least your mother didn't have to suffer and you didn't have to watch her body being slowly destroyed by cancer."

Another participant might respond, "But you got to say good-bye. At least you knew. I'd have given everything I had for ten minutes to say good-bye."

There is no better or worse death. Loss is loss, and the grief that follows is a subjective pain that only we will know. In sudden death, just like any other kind, the person left behind needs to take it day by day. But how do you find your way in the new, lonely, numbing world? Sometimes doing normal things gives you a sense of normalcy.

Phil did not really want to return to work after the sudden death of his wife, Kristen. His partner had told him to take all the time off he needed, but for sanity's sake, he figured he needed some structure in his life. Now he recognizes that "There had to be a part of my world that didn't die."

Phil found that with seeing friends and going to work he was able to survive. In time, others are shocked to find they do more than just survive, they actually enjoy life again.

Sonia shared, "I always wanted to be in a book club, but with work and marriage I never had time. When Jess died, I was devastated, but I realized that suffering through the rest of my life would not bring him back. I decided finally to join a book club, and I'm surprised at how much I love it. I didn't think I had much left to discover after Jess's death, but I was wrong."

People who have dealt with sudden death often have words that may trigger pain. It could be as common a word as "suddenly." Celeste often talks about how hard it is when someone just says, "Suddenly the cake was ready," or "Suddenly it was time to go to the movies." She is someone who knows the horror of what "suddenly" can really mean.

In deaths that are the result of a crime, there are still other unique elements of grief. There is a perpetrator, so the death could have been prevented. There is the trauma of how someone died that a person has to grieve, as they imagine their beloved being hurt and dying a horrible death with no one there to comfort them. This is where the justice system comes into play.

Did they find the perpetrator? If not, how can society be safe? Did the police do everything they could?

There is a lack of closure that blocks grief when the perpetrator cannot be found. When they are found, families of victims will tell you that the punishment rarely fits the crime, and in this way, the grief process becomes intertwined with our legal system. The randomness of a crime also leaves us reeling. Millions of people take money from an ATM at all hours of the day and night. Why did my best friend have to be the one who was robbed at gunpoint and shot to death? Everyone drives a car, so why did my son get killed by a drunk driver?

On a hot Sunday afternoon, a little girl of six asked her mother if she could go down to the corner store and get an ice cream.

"After you do your chores," her mother answered.

She did her chores and asked again.

"Okay," her mother said, "but just wait till your older brother gets home to take you."

He arrived home in an hour and agreed to take his sister to the store. She was happily eating her ice cream cone on the way home when she was hit by a random bullet and died on the spot. Who fired the gun and why was never answered, and her mother had to find a way to live with the random tragedy. She was angry at a blank-faced person who pulled the trigger on her daughter, so where should she direct the anger and regret? What if she had taken her daughter to the store when she first asked—would she still be alive? She will always wonder if different timing might have produced a different outcome. She will never know, but she will know all too well the agony of tragedy.

The idea of turning things around before the tragedy struck is a common fantasy in crime-related deaths. Survivors often find themselves reading the obituaries, scanning for people who are under sixty-five years old to see if they suffered a sudden death from an illness or a crime. They are looking for reassurance that such things happen to other people, too, as they try to compare sudden death causes.

In these cases, some people reach out for comfort, while others will keep their pain to themselves. But everyone will feel the depth of their loss.

Even with lots of warning and preparation, death is an unbelievably difficult event, and when it is sudden, it has its own set of complications. We all know that we will live and we will die, because we see beginnings and endings all around us in nature. We can accept intellectually that everything has its season and time. But it may be harder to find peace in a world that regards autumn as the time only when the ground is covered with old brown leaves.

How can we understand when green leaves fall?

5. The Changing Face of Grief

"You're not going to grieve forever, are you?" "How long does it take to get through those five stages?" "Haven't you grieved long enough?" "Isn't it time to move on and get over your loss?"

Unfortunately, these questions are frequently asked of those who have experienced a loss.

Grief is not just a series of events, stages, or timelines. Our society places enormous pressure on us to get over loss, to get through the grief. But how long do you grieve for a husband of fifty years, a teenager killed in a car accident, a four-year-old child: a year? five years? forever? The loss happens in time, in fact in a moment, but its aftermath lasts a lifetime.

Grief is real because loss is real. Each grief has its own imprint, as distinctive and as unique as the person we lost. The pain of loss is so intense, so heartbreaking, because in loving we deeply connect with another human being, and grief is the reflection of the connection that has been lost. We think we want to avoid the grief, but really it is the pain of the loss we want to avoid. Grief is the healing process that ultimately brings us comfort in our pain.

That pain and our love are forever connected. To avoid the pain of loss would be to avoid the love and the life we shared. C. S. Lewis said, "The pain now is part of the happiness then.

That's the deal." To deny that loss is to deny the love. And in order to cope with the enormous loss we feel after death, we often enter the stage of denial quickly. That "I can't believe it" or "not me" reaction is an important tool in coping with the loss that has occurred. In grieving we struggle to comprehend the loss of a loved one. Grief is a necessary step in going from death to life.

We plan for most everything in life. We plan weeks ahead for our birthday, months ahead for our vacations, over a year ahead for our weddings. We plan decades ahead for our retirement. But death, perhaps the biggest trip of our life, usually catches us by surprise. And when we lose a loved one to that unwanted mystery of life, we are never prepared.

Death is a line, a heartbreaking dividing line between the world we and our loved one lived in and the world where they now are. That line of death on a continuum becomes a Before and After mark. A line between time with them and time without them. A line that was drawn without us or our permission. An existence that continues for them but leaves us out, separating us from those we love and lose.

Healing grief is often an overwhelming and lonely experience. We do not have any real framework to help us recover from the loss of a loved one. We do not think we have the tools to overcome the feelings that devastate us. Our friends do not know what to say or how to help. As a result, during the days following a loss we wonder if we can survive. As time passes, that fear gives way to anger, sadness, isolation, feelings that assault us one after another. We need help.

Our generation saw death and grieving in a way no other generation ever had. John F. Kennedy became a familiar face with television. Though he was obviously not the first president assassinated, it was the first assassination captured on television for the world to watch. In that moment, in a way never possible before, we as a nation were bonded in a common grief. In that grief and loss, we remain bonded in a collective memory even today.

From the most personal to the public, we continue to be bombarded with images of national and international grief in a way we never could have imagined. From the loss of Princess Diana, Mother Teresa, John Kennedy Jr., and then, of course, the terrible events of September 11, we as a nation have been deluged with deaths that are "larger than life."

In these public losses and large memorials we feel like a community again. They are reminiscent of a time long past when we dealt with loss in a small town instead of our hospitals and funeral homes with relatives too far away to be a part of the loss.

Things were different a century ago. In death we gathered. We rang the town bell. A cooling board was put out for the body. Wood was collected for the casket. Fabric was sewn to dress the body. The loved one's body was put in the parlor. Everyone from the town gathered and paid their respects.

Everyone knew everyone else. Every visitor came with a story about our loved one. These stories created a rich tapestry. The person who presided over the memorial knew our loved one well and helped put the loss in perspective. Friends and family were all present at the burial site. Afterward they did things for us; they didn't ask what they could do or how they could help, they just did. There was no mystery of how to help another person in loss.

We live in a new death-denying, grief-dismissing world now. In America, we don't die well and we don't grieve well anymore. Illness moved into the hospital in the 1940s and death moved into the funeral home. We now, all too often, die among strangers. Only a few visitors at a time are allowed in the hospital room.

Hospice and palliative care are wonderful and yet still underutilized resources. We rarely gather as a family as our loved one dies. And if we do, the medical system forces us to do it in shifts. Children under fourteen are usually not allowed in hospitals.

If we mention our feelings of anticipatory grief to the doctor, he has a pill for us. At twenty-seven years old, what else has he to offer us? He has many demands on his time, as do the nurses. The doctors and nurses are caring and well meaning, but in a system designed to cure, there is no clear direction when someone is dying. We get the word from the nurse or doctor that our loved one has died, maybe even a quick phone call, sometimes with the same amount of emotion that you would find in a delivery notice. If we are there at the time of death, the nurses will help connect us with the mortuary.

We do not see our loved one until they magically appear again at the viewing or funeral, looking in death a way they never looked in life. We no longer routinely transport the dead in elegant black hearses; often we use white unmarked vans. We meet with a funeral director who handles everything in the funeral home. There is no town bell to ring, but he can put a notice in the paper. We don't know everyone in town anymore. We don't live in just one or two houses; in fact many of us will live in ten to twenty homes during our life. Our family will be spread out not over blocks but over states.

Ours is a productive society. Most corporations allow three to five days of bereavement. Very few, if any, will say, "Take as much time as you need, this is a very difficult time." Our work usually allows one death per year. After our bereavement time we must go back to our work. We may go back physically but not necessarily mentally. We are challenged to find closure and find it fast. We expect everyone to grieve the same way and in the same time.

But death doesn't have to be like that. You can choose to make the process more meaningful. As two people who have spent our lives dealing with loss and grief, we both visited concentration camps, where there are carvings of butterflies. They are an enduring symbol of transformation, that even in the face of great loss we will continue, someway, somehow. We spent time with Mother Teresa and witnessed the embodiment of human kindness. In our worst we have the power to find some thread of hope. In grief, just like in death, there is a transformation for the living. If you do not take the time to grieve, you cannot find a future in which loss is remembered and honored without pain.

6. Elisabeth Kübler-Ross: My Own Grief

JULY 17, 2004

I am no stranger to grief, although few people have actually seen me grieving. While I have made a career of dealing with death and dying, I came to my grief late in life. Having spent the last nine years partially paralyzed due to my strokes, I have often felt purposeless, even though I know I am still here for a reason. During this time I've had the opportunity to write two more books with my cowriter. There was something about having time to reflect and revisit old stories of loss that triggered my own.

The writing was cathartic, and as David and I talked through the work, there was something about my grief being witnessed by another that allowed it to rise to the surface. I cried many times during the writing of these two books. I had always experienced my work as the doer and creator. Now, being bedbound, I have felt the pain of all the lives and losses of which I had been a part. My life has always been integrated with death, but I had kept my personal grief at a distance. I have said many times that through my work I have come to realize that death doesn't exist. I am of course speaking spiritually and symbolically.

When a loved one dies, the reality of death on the physical level is all too real.

My first experience with this dramatic contrast between realities was when I was just eight years old. My parents thought I had a cold, but when it didn't get better I went to the hospital and was put in a room with a little girl about the same age as I.

In this world of people in white lab coats, I knew this little girl was sicker than I ever was. I also saw that she had no visitors. This little girl with porcelain translucent skin hardly said a word to me, but in her silence I understood a lot. After days together, she told me that she would be leaving later that night. I was concerned, but she said, "It's okay. There are angels waiting for me."

I had no fear about the journey my friend was going on. It was like the sunset. She appeared to die alone, but I felt she was attended to by others from another plane. While I felt she died without family and friends there, I did not feel much grief, because I had been reassured by her that it was okay. Even so, I thought it was a cold, lonely, sterile death.

In a few years I saw another death. My parents' friend, a farmer in his fifties, fell from an apple tree and broke his neck. The doctors said there was nothing they could do, and his family took him home to die. He had time for family and friends to visit while his bed was positioned to look outside the wide window at the flowers in the family garden. This kind of death had a peaceful, loving feeling, sad and yet warm, unlike the girl in the hospital. Naturally it is no surprise that in my last years I have been in a room with flowers and a big window to look out of.

My father, Ans Kübler, was a strong man who decided I was to be a secretary. My sister Erika was going to be an academic, and my sister Eva would receive general education.

But I was left with many questions: why was I born a triplet with no identity? It felt as if I'd been born with the loss of a single unique identity, because often my own parents couldn't tell us apart. I still have no idea why my dad was so tough and my mom was so loving, just as I will never know why I was born a two-pound "nothing" from Zurich.

Many people do not realize that I was famous at birth, but it was not a good kind of fame. Triplets like my sisters and me were on display since we were considered so unusual. You have to remember this was before infertility medications that caused twins and triplets and even quadruplets. All I knew was that our pictures appeared on billboards and I was invisible as an individual. To never feel that I uniquely mattered was a lesson that would help me recognize how much people meant to each other and how every loss, large and small, matters.

I also learned early on not to grieve for myself, not to cry and not to feel. During my childhood we always had bunnies around the house, and I loved each and every one of them. The problem was my father was thrifty, and every six months he needed to roast a bunny for our dinner. I would have to bring the beloved bunnies, one by one, to the butcher. But I always made sure that my own special bunny, Blackie, was never chosen. He was mine, the one love object I had that belonged only to me.

Blackie got pretty fat because I kept giving him extra food, and of course the dreaded day came when my father told me it was time for me to bring Blackie to the butcher. I could not allow it. I begged Blackie to run away, but the more I shooed him away, the more he thought I was playing and would run back to me. No matter what I did he kept coming back, and my pain only escalated when I realized that he loved me too.

The inevitable happened soon enough when my father sent me off with Blackie, making me promise to give him to the butcher. I did it, crying the whole time, and in a few minutes out came the butcher with my dead Blackie in a bag.

"Here's your rabbit," he said, handing it over. I felt catatonic when I reached out to accept it. I could still feel Blackie's warmth when the butcher remarked, "By the way, it's a damn shame you brought this bunny in now. It was a girl and in a day or two it would have had babies." That night at dinner when my family ate Blackie, in my eyes they were cannibals. But I would not cry for this bunny or anyone else for almost forty years.

It finally happened in a workshop in Hawaii. During the week, the landlord nickeled and dimed me for everything. For the next five days I felt unbelievable rage toward this man, so much so that I wanted to kill him. I struggled to contain the rage so it would not ruin the workshop, and when I arrived back home, my friends confronted me on my anger. After some resistance I talked out my anger and was shocked to suddenly find myself sobbing. The rage gave way to a deep sorrow underneath, and as I cried, I realized this was not only about the landlord. His cheapness had been the trigger that reminded me of my all-too-thrifty father. I was suddenly that little girl crying over Blackie. Over the next few days I cried for him and all the other losses that had gone ungrieved.

Perhaps the repression of my grief was instrumental in my reaching out to others to find their own. In this way I indirectly healed my own grief little by little. It is my profound desire that through this book other people will feel safer choosing a more direct method to heal their grief.

I think back to after the war when I was young and visited a concentration camp. I was overcome by sadness. The loss was in the air. I looked for something, anything that would help me understand. I looked for some sort of sign of how these people lived in the midst of such confining loss. As I walked through the huge barracks where people were housed in animal-like conditions, I noticed carvings on the walls. They'd written their names, dates, and anything to say they were there and did not want to be forgotten. There was one image repeated over and over again—the image of butterflies. I thought of all the places in the world where you might find butterflies, but never in a death camp. For the next twenty-five years I wondered why there were so many butterflies, and now I know that the butterfly is a symbol of transformation, not of death but of life continuing no matter what.

When I think of my own losses, I can see how I survived them. During my marriage to Emanuel Ross (Manny), I had a miscarriage, but I used my beliefs in a higher power to continue my life and work, undaunted. I then had a second miscarriage. Twice I had been accepted to a pediatric residency that I desperately wanted, and twice I was disqualified because I was pregnant. Because all the "good" residencies were taken, my only choice was a psychiatric residency. I was afraid I would be a woman who would always lose my babies, but life had other plans for me. A year later I had my first child, Ken, and then a second, Barbara. I see today that my life's work would not have been possible if it were not for this sad twist of fate. This mixture of loss and birth seemed a natural part of my life.

Another tremendous loss was the death of my ex-husband, Manny. Even after our divorce we remained friends and talked weekly. When he died I was devastated, since we had practically grown up together. He was the father of my children, and I have wonderful memories of our times together. One day my grown son, Ken, put on one of his father's suits and I could almost see Manny again. I also see characteristics of Manny in my daughter, Barbara, and my grandkids. I am struck in my own anticipatory grief how all my losses, even my own death, are intertwined with those who live on.

Years later, in 1994, I bought a three-hundred-acre farm in Virginia. I wanted it to be a place of healing, partially for the care of AIDS babies, and the locals were not happy with me. But I was used to stigmas around death and dying. I saw people dying of AIDS stigmatized the same way I saw people years before stigmatized by society. I had underestimated the hatred for my farm when, in the end, it was burned down by arsonists.

Since there was no use denying the loss of the farm, I accepted it. My life has been many things, but never easy. That is a fact, not a complaint, because I have learned there is no joy without hardships, no pleasure without pain. If not for death, would we appreciate life? I believe our purpose here is to love and be loved and grow. And having said that, there is no pain greater than the loss of a loved one. I have known from witnessing life that everyone goes through hardships. Adversity only makes you stronger. Life is hard, life is a struggle, like going to school where you are given many lessons. The more you learn, the harder the lessons get.

One of the other griefs I have to mourn is the modern medical system in which I find myself a patient. People have said I have denied or discounted my work. That is not the case. I now see it is my mourning the loss of true medicine and finding myself in a world where medicine is about management and not healing. Decisions are not made at the bedside of a patient but rather in an office by someone who has never seen the patient. I am saddened by the loss of the world of medicine I once knew.

I have expressed my sadness, my own grief that as I experience the system as a patient, there have been times I questioned whether I made a difference with my work. I realize in the big picture with all the wonderful patients I have worked with that of course I have. In the small picture, though, I witness the depersonalization of medicine, which I find disappointing and sad. For me, someone who has made a life in medicine, that is a true loss that I am still grieving.

Throughout my life I dreamed of a future where medicine would see the whole person and tend to all of their needs. And yet, even though I have more resources than many others, my insurance company allows only a certain number of physical therapy visits. Nothing is really based on my personal needs.

In 2002, one of my sisters, Erika, became very ill. I flew to be with her and offered her one of my kidneys to hopefully save her life. When she said something like, "If this is my time, then it is my time," it was easier to be angry than sad. As much as I intellectually understood, I still did not want my sister to die. In fact, I remember our childhood pact that we would always hang on to each other. At birth we came out so close together, I wondered if we would do the same in death. Once she was gone, I realized I was next, and that took me to a deeper level in my own anticipatory grief around my death.

I have been in anticipatory grief for years. This of all times in your life is the time to be your authentic self. Not what others think you should be or what the medical system thinks you should be but yourself, whether it is sad or angry. I now look out of my room as I get close to death. It has been a long time coming. I thought I would die a few years ago and I almost did. But I am still here because I need to learn patience and how to receive love. Being ill for nine years has forced me to learn patience, but I still struggle with receiving love.

I know death is close, but not quite yet. I lie here like so many people over the years, in a bed surrounded by flowers and looking out a big window. A room not much different from that first good death I saw. These last years have been like being stuck on a runway, not allowed to die and leave this earth, but not allowed to go back to the gate and fully live. I am reaching a greater understanding of the pain of anticipatory grief, which also gives me a greater understanding of my patients. In the meantime, I have my kids, my two wonderful grandkids, and I still love my work very much. Writing this book has given me a way to continue to feel useful in my life, even at its end.

The process of dying when it is prolonged like mine is a nightmare. I have struggled with the constant pain and paralysis. After many years of total independence it is a difficult state of being. It has been a long nine years since my stroke, and I am anxious to die—graduate, as I call it.

I now know that the purpose of my life is more than these stages. I have been married, had kids, then grandkids, written books, and traveled. I have loved and lost, and I am so much more than five stages. And so are you.

It is not just about knowing the stages. It is not just about the life lost but also the life lived.

7. David Kessler:
My Own Grief

When I was nine years old, my family was living on the Gulf Coast a few blocks from the beach, where hurricanes are a summer event. Every year there were new storms with new names, but they required the same preparations and inspired the same fears. In that particular year, 1969, Hurricane Camille changed my world forever.

Over a hundred of us spent that night under the steel porch of the elementary school gym, which had been converted to a shelter by the Red Cross. It was the loudest night of my life. I mostly remember the crashing sounds and the howling winds. I knew that there was death and destruction in that noise, and that somewhere out there cries for help were going unheeded.

Then, suddenly, there was nothing. No wind, no rain, no sound. Complete silence. We were in the eye of the storm. As the storm moved past us the winds started up again, this time from the opposite direction. As the howling and crashing sounds returned, we wondered how we could possibly survive the night.

As day broke I wondered what our house would be like. I hoped my parakeet, Blue Eyes, would be okay, but as we drove to the house, I didn't recognize where we were. When we rounded the corner of our street I saw concrete and water where the house next door should have been. The front yard of our house was filled with rubble, stones, and debris from other houses. Some of the trees were down and some had fallen on the side of the roof. When I saw that the front door and the windows were gone, I knew my parakeet, Blue Eyes, was in trouble.

I ran to my bedroom so fast and yet it felt like slow motion, since I was aware that there was no furniture and the floor was covered with mud. There was no bed, no cage, no place to look for my bird, Blue Eyes. I stood alone in my previously familiar room that was now filled with sadness. I didn't or couldn't imagine all that I had lost, but I could feel it. That was my first encounter with grief. I had lost my room, my bird, and my house. I had no idea where my neighbors were. All I could do was have endless discussions about "Surely a bird can survive in wind and fly away." I remember annoying my parents with question after question until I started having a sidebar with anyone who would listen.

Someone finally said to me quite harshly, "Don't you understand, David, that everything is smashed and ruined, the cage is gone, the bird could never have lived."

That hurt, but it helped. I didn't know why, but I could end my search and begin to feel the loss. With the help of the Red Cross, we were able to rent another house and rebuild our lives, but things would never be the same.

My mother had dealt with health problems throughout much of my childhood. On New Year's Eve of 1973 I walked into my mother's bedroom where she had been ailing. I gave her a kiss and said, "This will be the year you get better." Within days she was transferred from our small local veterans hospital to a much larger, better-equipped VA hospital.

My father and I stayed at a hotel across the park from the hospital, but we were mostly in the hospital lobby, since she was in an intensive care unit where she was allowed only ten minutes every two hours for visitors. One morning, we had just eaten at the hotel and were on our way to see my mom when there was sudden activity in the hotel lobby. People began running out. Shots were being fired. There was a sniper on top of the building. Within seconds, there were police everywhere while people rushed into the buildings for cover.

We eventually made our way over to the hospital and saw my mom for the ten A.M. visit. She died alone an hour later. The doctor very reluctantly agreed to let my father see her but said that I could not, for I was too young. My heart sank. When the nurse came to lead my father to Mother I went along, hoping not to be caught.

The nurse led us to Mother's bed, where her body now lay lifeless. I remember thinking how much more at peace she looked without all the tubes and machines attached to her. I also remember how removed from her I'd felt during those last visits, with an oxygen mask covering her face, three to four IV lines, and the dialysis hookup. Imagine how hard it would be for anyone, much less a child, to complete or say good-bye or have any kind of intimacy in this stark institutional setting.

I was relieved to at least be face-to-face with my mother without all the machines and tubes. Still, I felt little privacy, for the other seventeen patients in the ward were there. And the nurse stood right by us at my mother's body, never leaving us alone, prepared to whisk us out when our brief allotted time was up. Before the day was over we were on a plane heading to bury my mother. I never felt so alone.

I knew this was not how death was supposed to be. The loss was never really dealt with. There were a few times I saw my father crying and he found me crying also, but it was never talked about and we never cried together. Although I was too young to articulate it, I knew that my grief deserved a place but had none. Far from the average childhood day, there had been death, shooting, police, and airplanes. My little psyche had its hands full. So how does a child integrate all those things?

He doesn't. But it was a huge cost to me and my family. I didn't deal with it for years, and when I did, I was fortunate enough to choose a profession that was about my acknowledging and healing my grief by helping others through illness, death, and grief. Yet not everyone has the opportunity to channel their sadness and loss into a positive outlet. I am painfully aware of how easily my loss could have devastated my life. I saw many others who had similar experiences and ended up involved in drugs, crimes, and even suicide. I often felt that "There but for the grace of God go I." My career is living proof that we teach what we need to learn.

In my late twenties I visited the Auschwitz concentration camp. On that day my level of understanding of grief and loss stretched way beyond anything I had ever experienced. I saw thousands of pairs of children's shoes, old luggage covered with travel stickers and ID tags, eyeglasses, and other personal items. It was incomprehensible that there had been a person or child connected to each of these items. Standing safely in the gas chambers, where millions were killed, took me to a depth of sadness I did not know was possible. I had known only personal loss. Now I knew global loss. For months I felt angry. Later I realized that my anger was part of my grief.

In the mideighties I was working in home health care. The AIDS epidemic was growing and hospitals were not treating people well. Nurses were afraid to deliver food inside the hospital rooms for fear of catching something. They would leave meals at the door, and sick patients had to be well enough to get their own food or they didn't eat. The fear of AIDS often left patients medically as well as emotionally neglected. Early on there was no knowledge of necessary medical care, and there was also little human care.

Los Angeles was one of many epicenters of the epidemic, and the entertainment industry was hit hard. Home nursing care was the answer, since hospitals and hospices had reasons and a reluctance to step up to the plate. Hospitals didn't want people with a communicable disease of unknown origins in their beds. Hospices had a system that was built under the Medicare system for those over sixty-five years of age. AIDS patients were too young.

My agency, Progressive Nursing Services, took a lead in caring for men, women, and children with AIDS. I joined my friend Marianne Williamson when she decided to start a meals on wheels program, Project Angel Food, for people with AIDS, since once again, the existing meals on wheels program was designed for the elderly. Because of my work at the nursing agency and building Project Angel Food with Marianne, AIDS seemed to be all around me. It felt like a war zone. The people we served were dying, the people we worked with were dying, and our friends were dying. I was overcome by numbness and loss. I could not have sat around and just felt my grief; it would have been too overwhelming.

I was lucky I had a mission to put my work into. It was one of the saddest times of my life and the greatest opportunity I was ever given to serve. At its peak, I remember going to a funeral every weekend, where I learned the importance of memorials and how vital it was to have a time and place to grieve for each individual loss. People thought of AIDS as only a gay disease back then, but we knew differently because we were caring for women and children from the beginning. We knew this deadly virus did not care about who its host was and that it would spread rapidly here and in Africa and around the world.

It seems that when the universe wants to get your attention, it usually starts with the young men in a society. War is one example; AIDS is another. It somehow happens that to teach hard lessons, you must affect the vitality of an otherwise strong man, his mother, and the family. It taught me a lot about disenfranchised grief, which is grief that is unacknowledged and unvalued. Families would not show up to grieve their children dying of AIDS and disowned many of them at death. I remember calling the parents of a young man who had died of AIDS and informing them as gently as I could that their son had died. The father denied having a son. I thought I might have dialed the wrong number, when he said, "The moment our son said he had AIDS, he was not our son anymore." With that he hung up the phone and we were left to raise money for his burial.

And so, besides disenfranchised grief, I learned from AIDS that when you add a taboo to a death, the grief expands dramatically. In the midst of a global epidemic with which I was consumed, my father called from Sacramento and said, "I had a dream last night that I'm going to die soon. Can we spend some time together?"

When my father was facing death in the late 1980s, I was determined to have a better experience of death with him than I had with my mother. I brought my dad into my home, making sure that he was surrounded by loved ones and cared for at all times. My father talked openly about dying. My emotions were mixed. I was sad but also glad that he was prepared to move on with peace of mind. His openness and acceptance of the situation helped me find completeness with him that had not been possible with my mother. The anticipatory grief we shared brought us even closer in our relationship. I was able to lovingly hold his hand as he died. As a result, the grief around my father's death was easier to bear than that around my mother's.

By the midnineties, AIDS in the United States had become a manageable chronic illness rather than a death sentence, my parents were gone, and I had witnessed the worst of mankind at Auschwitz. I needed a way to express all the loss I had seen and felt. My first book, *The Needs of the Dying*, became that outlet. It enabled me to review all the aspects of loss of which I had been a part. But there was still something missing, something else I needed to heal—trauma.

I saw in my own loss that it was hard to separate out the grief from the trauma, since grief has elements of trauma in it and trauma has grief in it. I explored this by being trained and volunteering for the Red Cross's Aviation Disaster Team. I also became a specialist reserve police officer for their trauma team. Like a lot of other people, I was a product of my accumulated pasts and losses, which paved the way for who I have become today. That little boy who was not able to be with his mother when she died, saw police in action, and took his first plane ride all on the same day, the day that changed his life forever. That little boy back then sorely needed someone like the man I had become to help him. Like many in my profession—and other professions—my experiences and training were called forth on the saddest day in American history.

September 11, 2001, my phone rang, my beeper buzzed, and I received a fax from the American Red Cross stating that I, like so many other disaster volunteers, was being activated.

I knew there was a huge network in place that was being activated around the country to help. I wanted to get on the next plane to New York to be at Ground Zero, but all flights were grounded. The next call was from a friend who told me that my good friend Berry Berenson Perkins had been scheduled to fly from Boston to Los Angeles on one of the planes that crashed into the World Trade Center.

I went from shock, denial, and feeling that I had to get to New York to help, to being completely paralyzed. I couldn't do anything until I found out if Berry was alive. Not knowing if my friend was alive or dead and having no way to get to New York made minutes feel like hours.

I spoke with her son, who confirmed that Berry had indeed been on one of the planes that hit the World Trade Center building.

After I did my best to explain the situation to my two young sons, I began my work. I started meeting with grief-stricken pilots and flight attendants who had possibly lost coworkers and loved ones and were afraid to get back in the air. Within a few weeks, I was at Ground Zero and was told to help in the morgue.

On my way to the makeshift morgue I was struck by the grayness. It was like Auschwitz, but this was happening now. The smoke was in the air, the smell was horrifically overwhelming, and the grief was palpable. The shock of the morgue was that there were no corpses on the clean, unused tables. Each time a bell rang signifying a body had been found, everyone stopped. Some stood at attention, others prayed, and I braced myself for what I might see. The first time the chaplain brought me into the interior of the morgue for the arrival of a body, one finger was all that was brought in. The next day I met with a fireman's wife whose husband's body had recently been found. I knew nothing we had been through in our lives had prepared us for this experience. I was honored to be able to help.

As I recall the grief in my life, I think back to my first experience of death, my mother. I remember that little boy wanting to be with his mother as she died, but he wasn't allowed. A few years ago I had the opportunity to go back and visit the hospital where she had died twenty-five years before. I stood at the ICU door, which had not changed a bit, and cried. A nurse walked up to me and said, "Would you like to go in and visit someone?"

I looked at her kind face and said, "No. The person I want to see is no longer in there, but thank you so much for asking."

In my life, I continue to heal my own grief. It doesn't go away; I just learn to live with loss, and I am now able to honor and remember the past without pain. Just like Elisabeth, but decades later, I had the privilege of visiting Mother Teresa in Calcutta. I will never forget what she said to me: "Life is an achievement and death is part of that achievement. The dying need tender, loving care, nothing more."

It is that life and love, found and lost, that is also part of the achievement.

When we first lose a loved one, our lives feeling meaningless. As we experience the five stages of grief, we are returned to a life with the possibility of meaningfulness that was unimaginable when we first dealt with the loss. I believe that grief and its unique healing powers take us from meaninglessness to meaningfulness again. If there is a sixth stage, I would call it "meaningfulness," or "renewed meaning." We do not get over our loss, we don't find recovery; we may find renewed meaning and enrichment for having known our loved one.

In working with Elisabeth and experiencing my own grief, I am reminded of life's fragility. What I have taught in my life about grief is not as important as what I have learned from it: Those whom we have loved and who loved us in return will always live on in our hearts and minds. As you continue on your journey, know that you are richer and stronger, and that you know yourself better now.

You have transformed and evolved.

You have loved, lost, and survived.

You can find gratitude for the time you and your loved one shared together, as short as that seems to have been. Time helps as you continue healing and live on.

Yours is the grace of life, death, and love.

Afterword:
The Gift of Grief

Grief is the intense emotional response to the pain of a loss. It is the reflection of a connection that has been broken. Most important, grief is an emotional, spiritual, and psychological journey to healing.

There is wonder in the power of grief. We don't appreciate its healing powers, yet they are extraordinary and wondrous. It is just as amazing as the physical healing that occurs after a car accident or major surgery. Grief transforms the broken, wounded soul, a soul that no longer wants to get up in the morning, a soul that can find no reason for living, a soul that has suffered an unbelievable loss.

Grief alone has the power to heal.

Think of a time when someone close to you experienced an important loss. Think of his life following that loss. Then think of him a year later. If he grieved, a miraculous shift may have occurred. If a healing did not take place, it is most likely because he did not allow himself to grieve.

Grief always works.

Grief always heals.

Many problems in our lives stem from grief unresolved and unhealed. When we do not work through our grief, we lose an opportunity to heal our soul, psyche, and heart.

227

In today's culture there are so few models of grief. It is invisible to the untrained eye. We don't teach our children how to cope with loss. People don't say to their children, "This is how you heal after a loved one dies, this is how we mourn."

There are a few farsighted individuals. One woman came up after a lecture to tell how she brought her children to her own father's grave, their grandfather whom they barely remembered. She said, "I sat there and cried in front of them. I then told them a few stories about him and laughed before crying again. I told them this is what grieving looks like. I taught them everything else, why wouldn't I teach them how to grieve? I know they will experience loss and death in their lives, and I want them to be able to move through those feelings."

Few of us had parents who taught us this valuable process and modeled it for us. We will always remember Jackie Kennedy with her children, publicly mourning her husband and our president. In the aftermath of his death, she looked to a model of the past for guidance. She found her archetype in the funeral of Abraham Lincoln, which she followed for her own beloved husband. When it came to her own death, Jacqueline Kennedy Onassis again taught us how to conduct ourselves in the face of death. She died surrounded by her family and her books. At her funeral her son described three of her attributes: "love of words, the bonds of home and family, and her spirit of adventure."

Yet we are still left unguided. What happened to the grieving families after the funerals? What was their first grief like? How did they survive? To whom did they turn for support? How did they cope and heal?

While some mourners have access to bereavement counselors and other health-care professionals, most people today feel very alone in their grief. They long for a pathway through their pain and isolation. They unconsciously seek models, which are few and far between. They turn to family and friends who are often unfamiliar and uncomfortable with the grieving process themselves.

Not knowing how to handle the pain of grief, we avoid it, not realizing it is the pain of the loss we are trying to avoid. A pain that will strike, no matter how much we try to avoid it. Yet by avoiding grief we turn our backs to the help that grief offers, thus prolonging the pain.

Why grieve? For two reasons. First, those who grieve well, live well. Second, and most important, grief is the healing process of the heart, soul, and mind; it is the path that returns us to wholeness. It shouldn't be a matter of *if* you will grieve; the question is *when* will you grieve. And until we do, we suffer from the effects of that unfinished business.

Unfinished business encompasses all those things we haven't said or done. The feelings we wish we allowed ourselves to feel. Those feelings that we have ignored and not attended to. Unfinished business from old wounds and previous losses can resurface in our current grief. It makes our present grief feel overwhelming, bigger than the loss we are currently experiencing. For example, unfinished business from the loss of a father can reemerge at the funeral of a coworker whom we didn't even know well. Fortunately, unresolved pain always makes itself known and steps up boldly, if inconveniently, to be dealt with.

Grief is one of life's passages we all experience. It is one of life's equalizers, a shared experience for every man and woman who lives. But though it is a shared experience, most of us go through it as little islands of pain. Most of the people around us don't know how to help. We want help but probably wouldn't even know what that help would look like. We just know a major loss has taken place. We know we can't bring back that loss and we can't take away the pain. Our pain makes others very uncomfortable. Our pain reminds them of their own, it reminds them of how precarious their lives are too. It is their own pain and fear that cause others to say such things as "Get over it, already," or "It's been six months, are you going to grieve forever?"

At a lecture, a woman named Meredith shared her story. Meredith's friends were telling her she just wasn't herself—what was going on? She explained that it was the twenty-fifth anniversary of her mother's death. One of her friends naïvely asked, "It still upsets you twenty-five years later?" Meredith replied, "I don't fall apart and I do feel healed, but I don't forget." She remembers the mother she had and still grieves for the child who lost her innocence too soon.

The reality is that you will grieve forever. You will not "get over" the loss of a loved one; you will learn to live with it. You will heal, and you will rebuild yourself around the loss you have suffered. You will be whole again, but you will never be the same. Nor should you be the same, nor would you want to.

The time we take following a loss is important in grief and grieving as well as in healing. This gift of grief represents a completion of a connection we will never forget. A time of reflection, pain, despair, tragedy, hope, readjustment, reinvolvement, and healing.

The time after a significant loss is full of the feelings that we usually have spent a lifetime trying not to feel. Sadness, anger, and emotional pain sit on our doorstep with a deeper range than we have ever felt. Their intensity is beyond our normal range of human emotions. Our defenses are no match for the power of the loss. We stand alone with no precedent or emotional repertoire for this kind of loss. We have never lost a mother, father, spouse, or child before. To know these feelings and meet them for the first time brings up responses from draining to terrifying and everything in between. We don't know that these foreign, unwelcome, intense feelings are part of the healing process. How can anything that feels so bad ever help to heal us?

With the power of grief comes much of the fruits of our grief and grieving. We may still be in the beginning of our grief, and yet, it winds its way from the feelings of anticipating a loss to the beginnings of reinvolvement. It completes an intense cycle of emotional upheaval. It doesn't mean we forget; it doesn't mean we are not revisited by the pain of loss. It does mean we have experienced life to its fullest, complete with the cycle of birth and death. We have survived loss. We are allowing the power of grief and grieving to help us to heal and to live with the one we lost.

That is the Grace of Grief.

That is the Miracle of Grief.

That is the Gift of Grief.

Acknowledgments

We would like to extend our deepest gratitude to Frank Arauz for his unyielding kindness, care, and love of our mother. Frank allowed our mother to be "home" when she was not able to live in her own home anymore. We thank Barbara Hogenson for her many years of hard work and friendship. We thank David Kessler for his many years of friendship and his humor. Thank you, David, for your support of our mother and of us, when it was her time to go. Thank you, Brooks Cowen, for your compassion and support as we said good-bye. We would like to express our love and profound appreciation of our father, Emanuel R. Ross, M.D., for all he did to make it possible for us to share our mother with the world.

Mom—we thank you for giving us the invaluable gift of seeing the world through your eyes and the gift of a world that will never forget you . . . until we meet again.

—Kenneth Ross
and Barbara Rothweiler

How could I ever find the words to thank my coauthor, Elisabeth Kübler-Ross? She lives in the pages of this book as well as in my heart. Our writing two books together and all her guidance, from working with the dying and the bereaved to being my mentor in the writing and lecturing, have meant the world to me. Those gifts were more than I could ever have hoped for and more than I expected. Underneath it all was a love that was unique and magical in every way. I will always miss Elisabeth.

Elisabeth also gave me an added gift, getting to know her son and daughter, Ken and Barbara. Ken, thank you for taking care of the details and yet always seeing the big picture. And thank you for your photography and capturing so many wonderful moments for us.

Much appreciation to Susan Moldow at Scribner. Thank you for recognizing the need for this book and making it a reality. Thank you, Mitchell Ivers, our talented editor, who was truly there whenever we needed him. It is rare that authors get to choose their editor, but when given the opportunity, Mitchell Ivers was our only choice. Thanks also to Lucy Kenyon for getting the word out about the book and helping us reach so many. To Josh Martino and all our friends at Simon & Schuster and Scribner.

A special thanks to my agent Jennifer Rudolph Walsh at William Morris Agency. Also at William Morris: Tracy Fisher for her work on the book in so many other countries. My thanks also go out to Lisa Grubka, Katie Glick, and Michelle Feehan for their help along the way.

I could not have done a book like this without the support of many people. These words do not do your kindness and generosity justice. For my friend Andrea Cagan, who encouraged me, kept my hands moving across the keyboard, and kept me centered when I felt pulled in a million directions. Linda Hewitt, who truly cares about the quality of everything I do and is a gift in my life in more ways than I could possibly ever list.

My thanks to Lori Oberon, Michael Flesock, Garrison Singer, Susan Edelstein, Bonnie Geary, Deanna Edwards, and Melinda Docter. And to Harold Ivan Smith and Robert Zucker, who so generously share their wonderful work in the field of grief.

Thanks to those respected individuals who gave their time to review this manuscript for completeness. Bonnita Wirth, Ph.D., American Red Cross; Juanita Thompson, LCSW, Citrus Valley Hospice; Rosemarie White, Ph.D.; Fredda Wasserman, MFT, MPH; Michelle A. Post, MA, MFT; Freddi Segal-Gidan, PA, Ph.D., USC Keck School of Medicine and Co-Director, USC/Rancho Alzheimers Research Center; Rabbi Sheldon Pennes, Jewish Hospice Project; Father Patrick Brennan, CP, Mater Dolorosa Passionist Retreat Center; Reverend Mark Vierra, North Hollywood Church of Religious Science; Rabbi Alan Rabishaw, Stephen S. Wise Temple; Father Arthur Carrillo, CP; and Pastor Steve Austin, Lakewood Church.

And to my colleagues at Citrus Valley Health Partners and Citrus Valley Hospice: Thank you, Elvia Foulke and Carol Brainerd, for the opportunity to work in an environment that encourages and challenges me every day and reminds me what is important. To Tom Adams, Maria Alvarez, Patricia Bommarito, Carmen Carrillo, Sherrie Cisneros, Dolores Crist, Glenn Fortich, Renee Gaines, Rosemary Gallo, Ed Gardner, Digna Herrera, Janene House, Tom McGuiness, Louisa Parrish, Pam Porreca, Joseph Powers, Lourdes Salandanan, Chris Sanchez, Maria Sanchez-Dones, Lila San Nicolas, Dennis Strum, Juanita Thompson, Debbie Tracy, and Joan Wachtelborn.

And a special thanks to all my friends who got me through this project and through life: Adele Bass, Josefine Bloom, Frida Blomgren, Janine Burke, Nastaran Dibai, Annie Gad, Jeffrey Hodes, Ann and Curt Massie, Ed Rada, Warren B. Riley, Terri Ritter, Pam Saffire, James Thommes, Steve Tyler, Steve Uribe, Emma Williamson, and Marianne Williamson.

To my sons, Richard and David, who remind me daily that love is all that matters.

—David Kessler